SOCIAL WORK THEORY:

A STRAIGHTFORWARD GUIDE FOR PRACTICE ASSESSORS AND PLACEMENT SUPERVISORS

By:Siobhan Maclean and
Rob Harrison

Kirwin Maclean Associates Ltd

Social Work Theory:
A Straightforward Guide for Practice Assessors and Placement
Supervisors

By Siobhan Maclean and Rob Harrison

First Edition: **2008 ISBN: 978-1-903575-52-9**

A catalogue record for this book will be available from the British
Library

Kirwin Maclean Associates Limited, 47 Albion Street, Rugeley, Staffs
All Rights Reserved

ISBN: 978-1-903575-52-9

Printed in Great Britain by:
Kirwin Maclean Associates Limited, Rugeley, Staffordshire

CONTENTS

HOW TO USE THIS GUIDE

This Guide has been written to address the anxiety that Practice Assessors and Placement Supervisors often have about social work theory. As active practice teachers, we have tried to design this book to address the needs of all involved in practice learning in the following ways:

<u>Ideas for work with students</u>

Section A provides a range of ideas for discussing theory generally with students. It also provides a few general ideas for exercises which can be used with students to explore the application of theory to practice generally. In subsequent sections, further ideas for supervision discussion and exercises to use with students appear at the end of the explanation about every theory covered. There is no way that you could cover all of these with one student in one practice learning opportunity. You should only use those which you think will be useful and relevant. We have, however, provided ideas and questions to inform discussions following each theory covered, in order to develop practice assessors' confidence in discussing particular theories.

<u>Refreshing your own knowledge</u>

We have tried to briefly explore the major theories of social work in this Guide. Ideas are provided for further reading in most areas as this book only provides a brief outline. It is likely that none of the theories will be entirely new to you – but many practice assessors and placement supervisors feel that they are out of touch with the language and ideas expressed in social work theory. We hope that you will be able to use this Guide to refresh your knowledge.

<u>Use of the Index</u>

We have tried to design the index with the needs of practice assessors in mind. Sometimes when discussing theories with students in supervision, they don't necessarily use the 'title' of the theory which may be familiar to the practice assessor, but they use some of the language drawn from the theory – which can confuse practice assessors and raise their anxiety further. We have therefore included a range of the language involved in particular social work theories in the index – this should aid the practice assessor in quickly accessing the information they need to further develop discussions with students.

Using theory in the practice assessor role

We have, at times, briefly discussed how some of the theories covered in this Guide can guide your practice learning role with students. However, we have mainly focussed on the use of theory in social work practice. If you want to know more about using theory in practice learning, you may be interested in another of our publications - *Developing Quality Practice Learning in Social Work: A Straightforward Guide for Practice Teachers and Supervisors.*

A   THEORY AND PRACTICE LEARNING

Social work students often begin their practice learning experience intimidated by the idea of applying theory to their practice. Sometimes practice assessors and supervisors are even more intimidated by the idea of theory.

Requirements for the degree in social work make clear the need for students to apply theory to their practice. Students and practice assessors therefore need to address their varying concerns about theory.

Practice learning is about relating the ideas learned in University to the practice setting. However, in order to support a student to link their theoretical knowledge to practice, practice assessors need a firm grasp of the fact that theory is something everybody uses every day in social work and that theory has a clear link to common sense/what works/real life or whatever the phrase of choice is. Without this, theory can become something which seems abstract and the myth that it is something you learn at University and then forget when you enter the "real world" of work is perpetuated.

FURTHER READING

This Guide provides an introduction to the main theories of social work. Further reading will always be useful. For further information on the areas covered in this section, see the following:

- Beckett, C. (2006) *Essential Theory for Social Work Practice.* (London) SAGE.

- Dominelli, L. (2004) *Social Work: Theory and Practice for a Changing Profession. (Cambridge) Policy Press.*

- Fook, J. (2002) *Social Work: Critical Theory and Practice.* (London) SAGE.

- Payne, M. (2005) *Modern Social Work Theory.* Third Edition. (Basingstoke) Palgrave Macmillan.

- Thompson, N. (2002) *Theory and Practice in Human Services.* (Buckinghamshire) OU Press.

AN INTRODUCTION TO
THEORY AND PRACTICE

Theories in social work are nothing more than an attempt to explain situations and social relationships. Theories have been developed since it became clear that there were similar patterns or repeating cycles of behaviour both in an individual's life and in the lives of lots of different people. Since theories have been expressed by academics and social scientists, they often use an academic language. Don't let that put you off. Theories are life dressed up! Many theories actually have a very straightforward, accessible message, even if sometimes you have to look beyond the jargon.

If theory is to be useful then it needs to have a clear link to experience. Einstein who developed what is probably the most famous theory of all – the theory of relativity – said:

"A theory is the more impressive the greater is the simplicity of its premises, the more different are the kinds of things it relates to and the more extended the range of its applicability."

(www.thinkexist.com 2005)

There has been some debate about what actually constitutes a theory. Generally, a theory helps to explain a situation and perhaps how it came about. In science, a theory is seen as helping to:

➢ describe (eg: what is happening?)

➢ explain (eg: why is it happening?)

➢ predict (eg: what is likely to happen next?)

Sometimes theories are also seen as helping to control a situation and bring about changes.

In supervision discussion, placement assignments, portfolios etc students should be able to describe the situation they are working with, explain why they think this came about, what they can do to bring about change etc. In doing so, they will be drawing upon some form of theory. They may, however, not be aware of this. This is where the practice assessor's skills in questioning and supporting a student to translate theory into practice are vital.

In social work, there are a range of different types of theory. An understanding of these different types or forms of theory can be helpful in supporting a student to recognise their use of a range of theories in any given situation.

Types of Theory

Beckett (2006) separates theory into 'formal' theory and 'informal' theory. Some people use these terms inappropriately – formal theory is taken to mean theory which is presented more academically, and informal theory is taken to mean theory which is more accessible and understandable (and therefore not academic!). However, this is a misunderstanding. Formal theory is the theory that we will cover in this Guide (and there is more) – it is basically theory which can be named and traced back to a writer or an academic. Informal theory on the other hand, is the worker's own ideas about a situation. As this is often developed through experience – both practice experience and personal experiences, this type of 'theory' is also referred to as practice wisdom (Doel and Shardlow 1993). Beckett (2006) also refers to informal theory as "common knowledge". It is our view that very often a workers 'practice wisdom' or 'common knowledge' usually contains a range of formal theory – although often the worker uses their own language to explain this, rather than the language of the theory.

Whilst Beckett categorises theory into formal and informal, other writers draw other distinctions. One common idea is that there are theories *of* social work and theories *for* social work. In straightforward terms, this means that there are theories about the way social work is delivered which constitute theories *of* social work – e.g.: task centred practice, crisis intervention etc. Theories *for* social work are essentially theories which can explain situations, behaviours etc – such as behavioural approaches, systems theories etc.

Sibeon (1989) takes this idea further and proposes a three part distinction between theories:

➢ Theories of what social work does

➢ Theories of how to do social work

➢ Theories of the client's world

We have used Sibeon's ideas of the distinction between theories to try and place the theories in this Guide into Sections.

With many different types of theory, a worker can call on different theories to help them in different aspects of their work role. For example a worker may call on some *formal theory about the client's world* to help them to understand what is happening for the service user, they may then draw on some *informal and formal theory* about *how to do social work* to plan their intervention. In presenting a case for resources to their manager, the worker may draw on all of these and some *formal theories* about *what social work does*. So in dealing with one service user's situation, a worker is likely to draw on a whole range of theory. Whether or not they can necessarily name the theory is another matter.

Why do we need to apply theory to practice?

Whilst individual social work theories have different purposes, using all kinds of theory in our work offers us, as social workers, some important things. Sometimes students feel they don't need to apply theory to practice and practice assessors may need to explore this with students. Covering the following points with a student can be helpful in moving forward:

➤ Theories can help us to make sense of a situation. Using theory, we can generate ideas about what is going on, why things are as they are etc.

➤ Using theory can help to justify actions and explain practice to service users, carers and society in general. The aim is that this will lead to social work becoming more widely accountable and ultimately more respected.

➤ In work with individuals, making use of the theories which may relate to their specific situation will give us more direction in our work with them.

➤ Using theory can give a reason about why an action resulted in a particular consequence. This can help us review and possibly change our practice in an attempt to make the consequences more effective.

It is clear then, that theory is important in practice – both for work with service users and for social work to be more valued in society.

However, despite the fact that there are very clear reasons to apply theory to practice, practice assessors still have a range of concerns about the application of theory to practice learning.

Concerns about theory and practice

Those involved in practice learning may have concerns about the links between theory and practice for a range of reasons.

Many practice assessors and supervisors have been qualified for some time and think that they no longer use theory in their practice – they may think that they have forgotten the theory, that they now work on common sense principles, that they no longer have time to think about theory etc. We would challenge that by saying that everyone in social work is using theory on a day to day basis. They may simply not recognise this, it has seeped into their "common knowledge."

In terms of the claim to work on common sense principles – whose sense is common? Is your sense the same as everyone else's? Just because someone cannot imagine another way to view something doesn't mean that they aren't using theory. It just means that their one or two theories are their entire world or "sense".

Where practice assessors and supervisors are not from a social work background, they may have even more significant concerns about theory and practice. However, in many ways social work theory is drawn from a range of areas and disciplines and workers from other backgrounds are often surprised at how familiar they are with many aspects of social work theory.

Whatever the reason that practice assessors and supervisors are concerned about linking theory and practice, the fact remains that students need to be supported to link theory to practice and this is a key role for a practice assessor.

FACILITATING LEARNING ABOUT THEORY AND PRACTICE

The Requirements for Social Work Training state that all social work programmes must:

"Ensure that the teaching of theoretical knowledge, skills and values is based on their application to practice."

(Department of Health 2002:3)

Whilst the basic aspects of social work theory should be taught in the University setting, the practice assessor will need to help the student to transfer their knowledge and apply theory to their practice.

Practice assessors should be familiar with the practice learning environment and they should work to develop their understanding of the student's learning needs and styles. What they may not be so confident about, for the reasons covered in chapter one, is the theory base of social work. In order to assist a student to develop their understanding of theory informed practice, a practice assessor will need a level of confidence about theory:

"When we teach, we teach something to somebody. We need to know both our subject and student."

(Wilhelm et al 2001)

Sections B - F of this Guide outline some of the main theories in social work to familiarise or remind practice assessors and supervisors of the relevant theory base. The remainder of this section provides ideas about how to support students to recognise the application of these theories in their practice.

Just as there is no single approach to applying theory to practice, there is no single approach to supporting a student to learn about the application of theory to practice. What works will be different for each student, each practice assessor and each agency setting. Within this Guide we will attempt to use a "belt and braces" approach by going through some ideas in this section, and by suggesting possible "tips" by way of activities and discussion points to use with students throughout the remaining sections of the book.

Whenever you are discussing the application of theory to practice
with students, remember the following points:

➢ No single theory can explain everything. An eclectic approach is
usually required (see Section G).

➢ Different professionals may draw on different theories given the
same presenting situation. There is no right or wrong approach –
just boundaries of good practice.

➢ Theories of different types may be used at different points in
intervention in a case/situation.

➢ Some theories may compliment each other, but others may clash
and may therefore not be appropriate to use together.

➢ It is important to recognise that some theoretical approaches don't
work with some people. Applying Brief Solution Focussed Therapy
can be really effective with some people. For other people, it
leaves them cold.

➢ Students should take a critical approach to theory. If it doesn't
"work", why not? Can they adapt aspects so that it is helpful?

➢ Always apply the value base of social work to theory – much of the
theory used within social work is drawn from outside the
profession. Theory may have its roots in education, psychology or
management. As such, it may not incorporate social work values
and you should ensure students take responsibility for applying
these.

➢ An anti-oppressive approach is always vital – students should
critically evaluate any theory they choose to use from an anti-
oppressive standpoint.

A good working knowledge of theory is based on the perspective that
each service user is different and different approaches will be suited
to individual circumstances, needs and cultural requirements.
Students need to have a good "toolkit" and understanding of the
application of various approaches to ensure this anti-oppressive
individualised approach is something they continue into future
employment.

Students also need to be able to describe the actual application and
use of theories rather than just getting into a habit of listing theories
when asked about their decision making. Experienced practice
assessors will know how it can go: In supervision, the student and

practice assessor are discussing a situation the student has worked with and the practice assessor asks the student "what theories were you using?" once the petrified look has gone from the student's face, they say "task centred practice and attachment". The practice assessor says "OK". Box ticked. Nothing further. That's not applying theory to practice – it's plucking a few phrases from a book.

The aim should be for the student to be able to describe:

➢ What they did
➢ Why they did it
➢ <u>How</u> they applied each theory
➢ What worked and what they might do differently in their application of a theory in future
➢ What other theories may have been relevant to a situation or individual and why they chose not to use these

This is what makes the difference between someone who is studying for a professional qualification in social work and one who acts on instinct or "gut". If someone is professionally qualified, there is an expectation that they act ethically, with knowledge of why they make certain decisions, and that they are able to justify these, to managers, other professionals, vulnerable people and their families.

There needs to be scope within supervision sessions for reflection on decision making processes in relation to the use and application of theory. This is essential so that students can discuss their choices and means for coming to a decision. There also needs to be scope for theory to be something dynamic which is open to critique, as a worker who accepts everything which is "known" is not one who is thinking through application fully. A competent practitioner is one who makes informed choices with knowledge, understanding and conscious reasoning.

It is important for the practice assessor to ensure that students have opportunities to observe other workers putting theory into practice through their assessments and interpretations of need. This will enable the student to build their own confidence to try what works for them and to move away from the concept of theory as something purely academic and taught, to something which is used by everyone in the field.

Every learning opportunity a student has provides the scope for facilitating a student's learning about theory. A skilled and reflective practice assessor will make full use of coaching questions to enable a student to fully consider the theoretical approaches used. Theory needs to be constantly on the practice assessor's agenda to model theory informed practice for the student.

Students need to be able to move quite quickly in their ability to transfer the skills of learning about theory to future placements and work contexts. Allowing a range of activities and experiences, and focusing on building the student's confidence in discussing theory should work to achieve this.

We will discuss constructionism further in Section B, but it is useful to note that each and every agency a student will be placed with is in itself and its functioning a socially constructed notion based upon societal assumptions about need, risk, provision, ethics and individuality. Students are in a really unique position as team members delivering services, but with the ability to stand outside the construction of the service and reflect on why things are done in certain ways, what works, and how a service aims to meet peoples' needs.

A good example of this could be a placement in a Children's Centre where students could be enabled to reflect on:

➢ The aims of the service

➢ Whose needs the service meets (parents', agencies', society's)

➢ The positioning of the service within political agendas

➢ Discourse around employment, parenting, child development and rights

➢ Service delivery from a range of professional specialisms (commonality and difference)

Supporting students to understand that theories which may initially sound complex and difficult to apply, such as in this example, will enable them to reflect on where they want to position themselves in terms of future employment. It will support the development of critical thinking and analytical skills, which are again relevant to the professionalisation agenda and part of every degree course. There will also be benefits to the agency and the practice assessor in seeing things from a different point of view when a student is enabled to offer a critique. Finally, and arguably most importantly, allowing students to reflect on the best theory can offer and its application to different contexts will ensure future social workers are radical, creative and challenging professionals.

EXERCISES AND TECHNIQUES TO USE WITH STUDENTS

3

We always take a belt and braces approach to supporting a student's learning about theory and we use the same approach in this Guide. This chapter will provide some ideas on general exercises to use with students to enable their learning about the application of social work theory. Subsequent sections of the Guide provide some ideas for supporting students' learning about specific theories.

Theory Circles

We find that the use of theory circles can really help students who are struggling with the idea of theory. The idea is to place theory into a circle which, in many ways, reflects the social work process.

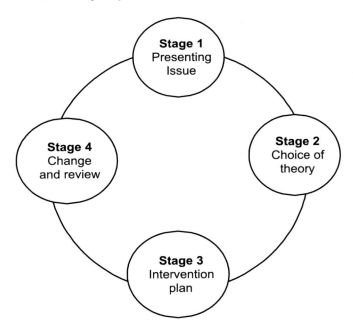

When a worker considers any presenting issue and decides on a plan of intervention, they have used a theory of some kind. They may not always be aware of it – but they have. To provide some examples of theory circles, we have chosen to reflect on a situation where a worker is working with a service user who has behaviour which is described as challenging or difficult to manage. The worker could take a variety of approaches, each of which would be informed by a different choice of theory. The following theory circles will help to illustrate the point:

Example 1:

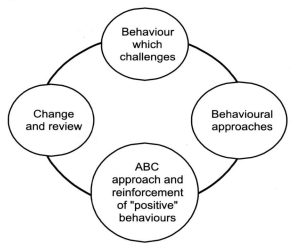

Example 2:

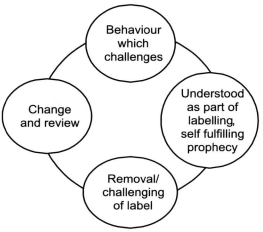

Example 3:

Example 4:

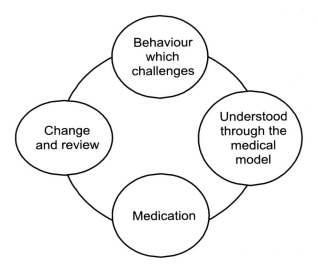

Example 5:

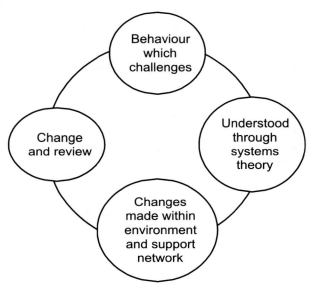

Example 6:

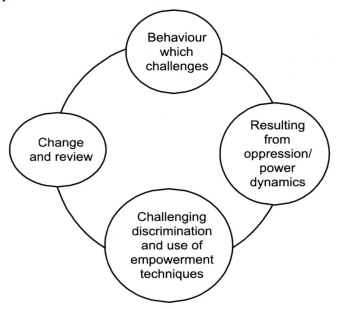

Many more examples could be given! The basic point we are trying to illustrate is that whatever intervention is planned is a result of the application of one theory or another. Many workers go straight from Stage 1 to Stage 3 in the "theory circle". Reflection and, if necessary, some research and knowledge development should help the student identify Stage 2 so that they can easily answer the dreaded question "and what theory are you using there?"

We said earlier that some theories appeal to some people and the same theories leave others cold. The same principle applies to theory circles – some students find theory circles very useful in understanding how theory informs practice – others don't.

Using bullet points/key issues to identify theory

Another exercise which can be useful to help students identify relevant theories is to encourage them to identify key areas through the use of bullet points.

When a student is working with a service user, ask them to identify:

➢ some key aspects of the service user identity

➢ key aspects of the presenting issues

➢ key aspects of agency context and practice

➢ key points of the work to be undertaken

For example:

copyright© Kirwin Maclean Associates Limited

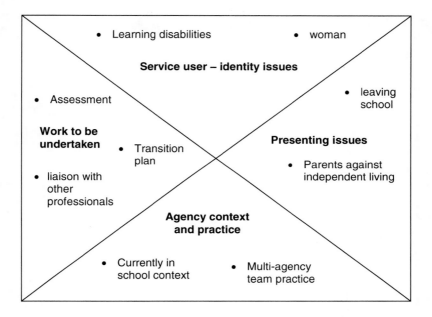

Helping the student to identify key points can help them to make the link with which theoretical approaches may be helpful. In the situation given as an example, the following theories may be relevant:

➢ Service user identity issues
  • Woman – feminist perspectives
  • Learning disability – social role valorisation; social/medical model; PCS model; understanding stigma and oppression etc

➢ Presenting issues
  • Empowerment; learnt helplessness; social learning theory etc

➢ Agency context and practice
  • Models of intervention
  • Multi-agency approaches
  • Social/medical approaches
  • Constructionism

➤ Work to be undertaken
  • Models of assessment, person centred planning etc....

Using an approach such as this may help a student to identify
relevant theories – discussion will still need to take place about the
detail of application etc.

Exercises which may help students to explore how they
apply theory to their practice and to become more confident
in this area:

➤ Apply the theory circle to one of your cases/pieces of
  work. Can you identify the theory/theories you have
  used to plan your intervention?

➤ Use the bullet points approach. How many theories
  might be applicable? Which ones have you used? How
  did they inform your work? Why did you choose not to
  use other possibly relevant theories?

➤ Use a reflective diary/ learning log to reflect on
  situations/ cases you found difficult/ interesting. Try
  to identify any theories you have used, or that were used
  by others.

➤ Keep a separate sheet for theories you have used and
  discussed in your work. List each as you use it. Some
  repetition will probably occur. Can you see which theory
  you use most? Why do you subscribe to that one more
  than others?

B

MODELS FOR UNDERSTANDING PEOPLES SITUATIONS: ANTI-OPPRESSIVE PRACTICE

We come from the position that all practice in social care and social work should be underpinned by a commitment to anti-oppressive practice.

Social work students need a clear sense that values and anti-oppressive practice are linked in with all the theory they will study and apply. Students should learn that all contact with people, all assessments, all planning and all subsequent interventions need to be approached with the principles of anti-oppressive practice at the forefront.

This section will support practice assessors to refresh themselves about theories around anti-oppressive practice. A grasp of the oppression and discrimination which people experience is fundamental to understanding the individual's world. Students need to be able to understand and analyse how society constructs notions of difference, and how people function within society as a result of this construction. This understanding has to be there for any worker to be able to assess and plan in partnership with an individual what could support them. This section is therefore about both theories of what social work does and theories about the client's world.

Reading this section will give a broad perspective around:

➢ The PCS model
➢ Social and medical models
➢ The Recovery Model
➢ Social constructionism
➢ Social Role Valorisation
➢ Discourse analysis
➢ Feminist perspectives
➢ Black perspectives

FURTHER READING

This Guide provides an introduction to the main theories of social work. For further, more detailed information on the areas covered in this section, see the following:

- Banks, S. (2001) *Ethics and Values in Social Work.* Second Edition. (Basingstoke) Palgrave.
- Barnes, C. and Mercer, G. (2003) *Disability.* (Cambridge) Policy Press.
- Beckett, C. and Maynard, A. (2005) *Values and Ethics in Social Work: An Introduction.* (London) SAGE.
- Burke, P. and Parker, J. (2006) *Social Work and Disadvantage: Addressing the Roots of Stigma through Association.* (London) Jessica Kingsley Publishers.
- Dominelli, L. (1997) *Anti-Racist Social Work.* (Basingstoke) Palgrave.
- Dominelli, L. (2002) *Feminist Social Work Theory and Practice.* (Basingstoke) Palgrave.
- Laird, S. (2008) *Anti-oppressive Social Work: A Guide for Developing Cultural Competence.* (London) SAGE
- Martin, E. and Martin, J. (1995) *Social Work and the Black Experience.* NASW Press.
- Parton, N and O'Byrne, P. (2000) *Constructive Social Work: Towards a New Practice.* (Basingstoke) MacMillan.
- Thompson, N. (2005) *Anti-Discriminatory Practice.* Third Edition. (Basingstoke) Palgrave.

THE PCS MODEL

4

Developed by Thompson (eg: 2005) the PCS Model offers a method to analyse the way that oppression operates and how it impacts on service users. The model proposes three levels (P, C and S as follows) which closely relate to each other.

P – personal or psychological
C – cultural
S – structural

Personal/Psychological

This basically refers to individual oppression – where an individual's thoughts, attitudes and actions sustain a broader pattern of discrimination.

Thompson explains that the P also refers to prejudice and practice – in that an individual worker's practice will reflect their personal views and their prejudices.

Cultural

Thompson explores the way that groups share common values, based on which they reach a consensus about what is "normal". Conformity to these constructed social norms is expected by groups. Where people don't conform, they may be segregated by the 'group'.

Thompson also outlines the way that comedy/comic humour is used to maintain these norms. Humour is often used as a mechanism of oppression and people are often "expected" to fall in with jokes which may sustain stereotypes and challenging these can be frowned upon as negatively "PC".

Structural

Thompson states that there are a range of structural social divisions which are closely related to power dynamics. Within society oppression is *"sewn in"* at an institutional level within the detail of society. Thompson refers to wider social forces and the socio-political dimension of the way difference is viewed by society.

Thompson proposes a diagrammatic representation of the model, as follows:

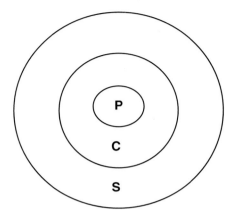

This is designed to show the way that personal prejudicial feelings are deeply embedded within cultural influences and structural forces. Hence personal oppression is reliant on cultural groupings and structural forces, whilst structural forces and cultural norms would not be upheld without personal prejudices.

This model gives an explanation of the strength of oppression and processes of socialisation and internalisation. It can be useful to help explore the nature of the oppression faced by service users. It is only in understanding the oppression that a worker can seek to challenge this. Students need to develop their confidence and skills in exploring the way oppression operates in order to support service users to understand and challenge the oppression they may face.

Many of the theories covered in the remainder of this section build on the PCS model. For example, constructionist approaches explore the way that social norms are constructed (as in the C of the PCS model).

Ask the student to prepare for a supervision session by reading up on the PCS model and applying this to a service user who they are working with.

Discuss with the student:

> How each layer of the diagram on the previous page may be constructed for that individual?

> Which elements and oppressions could be challenged by the provision of resources for that individual?

> How do wider changes within society occur?

SOCIAL AND MEDICAL MODELS   (5)

With an increased emphasis on joint working, it is helpful to have a clear understanding of the impact of social and medical perspectives on service users' situations. Workers from different professional backgrounds may share some views, and some may be quite different from a social work perspective. These perspectives are sometimes referred to as the social discourse and the medical discourse or more commonly as the social model and medical model.

Within every branch of social care and social work with children and adults, social and medical perspectives each put forward their own interpretation of why a person is in the situation they are.

The Medical Model

The medical model has developed since the mid 19th Century and this perspective locates the difficulty within the individual; they have an illness (physical or mental), an impairment or a type of personality that results in them being in the situation they are in. Through medical intervention the person can be cured or their difficulties lessened. Identification (diagnosis) of the illness or condition is by a doctor who also knows the cure.

➤ The medical emphasises a "normal" mind and a "healthy" physique. A person's impairment, disability or mental health problem is a deviation from the normal and needs to be corrected.

➤ The individual with the disability or impairment or mental health issue is the problem. This problem needs to be cured or corrected. This is often referred to as pathologising the individual.

➤ The impairment, disability or mental health problem is viewed as intrinsically bad or undesirable. Having a disability is seen as suffering a personal tragedy. This aspect when seen separately, can be referred to as the tragedy model of disability.

➤ Knowledge and expertise is located within the medical profession and the subsequent hierarchy. They know what is best for the person. This knowledge is made inaccessible to others by a language that is confusing. Words or phrases include:

- Diagnosis – what is wrong with the person
- Prognosis – likely outcome eg: cure or learn to live with the condition
- Aetiology – cause or origin of illness
- Pathology – change occurring due to illness or disease

➢ The disability, impairment or mental health problem has to be diagnosed. This is a form of labelling. The label is viewed very negatively in society.

➢ The person with the impairment or disability or mental health problem has to fit into society (as it is) and if they can't, then they are excluded or removed.

The Social Model

The social perspective views problems as located within society or the environment rather than an individual. This model of disability was generated in the 1970s and has progressively evolved. Aspects of the social model include:

➢ The concept of 'normal' is misleading and unhelpful. Instead there should be recognition that diversity is part of our human condition. This diversity should be celebrated and embraced, not treated.

➢ The social model draws a distinction between impairments (a recognition that a part of the body is not functioning) and disability. A person with an impairment is disabled (prevented from doing things) by society.

➢ Society disables people due to viewing their impairment negatively and then comprehensively discriminates against people with an impairment.

➢ People with a physical disability have been made invisible or ignored by society.

➢ The social model has made clear that society can make itself accessible to all people and disabled people have a right to equal opportunities.

➢ The social model has worked to counter the negative stigma associated with the labels applied to people. This is in a similar way to how other liberation movements have worked. For example, gay pride has been mirrored in the disabled people's movement.

> The social model has championed the expertise of the individual. Only the person themselves knows what is best for them. This can be particularly important where someone has medication, since side effects can be very individual.

<u>Continuing Debate</u>

Many people merge aspects of the medical and social models. Many doctors recognise the limitations of medication and other medical interventions. It is not unusual for a doctor to enter into a discussion with the patient as to what is the best way to proceed. There can be more shared decision making.

Unfortunately there are many social workers who are in awe of the medical profession and its power. If social workers are working with a service user who they find challenging, it is not unusual for them to look to a doctor for a cure or at least relief (in the form of medicating the service user).

Social workers need to maintain the view that many service users who challenge services have experienced broken relationships, difficult social circumstances and powerlessness. As such, students and workers could base their response more on the social model rather than the medical model.

The Application of the Social and Medical Models to Service User Groups

<u>Disability</u>

For most of the Twentieth century, the medical perspective was the dominant discourse in the care of people with a disability. People with physical disabilities and people with learning disabilities were diagnosed by doctors and if they couldn't be cared for in the family home were placed in services called hospitals which were staffed by nurses and doctors. In these hospitals some research was conducted which today would be considered voyeuristic and intrusive.

It is in the area of disability that, arguably, the social perspective has had the greatest success in displacing the medical perspective. People with a physical disability have been particularly active in promoting a social model perspective. The introduction of legislation making it a duty to maximise access is a sign of the success of the disability movement. This shows that if society wants to, it can make itself accessible. However, some people with a physical disability also acknowledge the strengths of the medical model – if they experience pain for example, they may value the involvement of medical staff and their advice about pain management.

Sexual Orientation

In 1992 the World Health Organisation finally removed homosexuality as a medical diagnosis from their classifications. Recently some medical research suggests that there may be a biological basis for some people being homosexual. However the medical perspective in the 1960s (male homosexual sexual activity was illegal until 1967) was that homosexuality was a treatable illness. Individuals were subjected to aversion treatment regimes intended to 'cure' the person of their homosexuality. Even after male homosexual sexual activity was made lawful, medical 'treatment' programmes were still available.

The gay and lesbian community has made clear their right to live their lives as they wish to. The call to respect diversity has been given significant support with the societal move towards equality for all.

Attention Deficit Hyper-Activity Disorder (ADHD)

One of the more recent areas of debate around the social and medical models has been caused by the increasing diagnosis of children with ADHD. There is an established professional view that ADHD is a definable medical condition which is treatable by medication and management techniques by parents and teachers. Others would suggest it could be symptomatic of a child's response to their environment (for example, poor and inconsistent parenting, sense of (in) security and stimulation/ activity)?

From the medical perspective:

➢ There is a list of symptoms that a doctor will ask the parents to comment on. A child would need to exhibit symptoms to an extent that is unusual for a child of that age, for a period of six months.

➢ There is no clear cause for ADHD. The child's temperament and genetic factors have been suggested. Diagnosis is made by a doctor after consultation with the parents and the child. The doctor may also involve a psychologist, health visitors etc.

> Treatment could involve medication. Ritalin is probably the most
well known but there are others. As with all medications and their
use by children, there is concern within the medical community
that it should not be used for indefinite periods.

From the social perspective, various questions are raised about
ADHD:

> The diagnosis of ADHD is a clinical diagnosis. This means a
doctor draws together all the information and makes a best
(informed) guess. There is no definable, definite marker for ADHD.
There is no blood test, no scan, no X-ray that can detect ADHD.
The doctor is particularly reliant on the parent's viewpoint.

> It appears that many children with the diagnosis of ADHD are in
families where there is a history of domestic violence. Some of the
symptoms of post-traumatic stress disorder and the symptoms of
ADHD are similar (e.g.: effects on ability to concentrate). The
social perspective argues that the effects of domestic violence on a
child are significant.

> Many children with the diagnosis of ADHD are in families where
the parents have not created and sustained strong attachments
with the child. Therefore the child could be displaying attachment
anxieties.

> It appears that in the last twenty years parental concern about how
dangerous the world is outside the family home has meant that
children have been brought into the home. The main parental
anxieties are around roads and the perceived risk of child
abduction and murder. If this is true (that children are not allowed
to play out as much as in the 1960s) then children have to expend
their energy in the home rather than run around outside.

> It is not clear if there is any social economic influence on the
prevalence of children diagnosed with ADHD. Are children
diagnosed with ADHD disproportionately drawn from poor
families?

> Following diagnosis of ADHD one of the principle interventions is
management techniques. This is code for applying good parenting
practice. If good parenting practice 'cures' a child of ADHD then is
it really a medical problem?

The social perspective towards ADHD raises questions rather than
promotes a cast iron alternative. It is possible that some children are

rightly diagnosed with ADHD. The social perspective would certainly raise concerns about the increasingly common use of the diagnosis and ask is it, at times, being used inappropriately?

<u>Mental Health</u>

Arguably, it is in the area of mental health that the social and medical perspectives have had the most significant debate.

The traditional medical perspective has a certain strength in its claims of clinically definable diagnosis. There are specific patterns of behaviour and expressed emotional states that can be given a specific diagnosis.

The medical perspective would argue that many mental health conditions are caused by metabolic or chemical imbalances in the brain. The chemical imbalances result in the brain's functioning being adversely effected and altering the person's perceptions of contact with people and in some cases, generating perceptions of voices or events that other people (who do not have the mental health condition) do not experience. In general the medical perspective would claim that most conditions can be treated. Treatment could include a range of interventions. The most 'medical' being medication. However, other treatments are available and could include talking therapies (such as counselling or psychotherapy and cognitive behavioural therapy) and opportunities to find mutual support from self help groups etc.

The social perspective has been developed in the last thirty years or so. Many people have contributed to this development which has many aspects.

One of the points raised by the social perspective on mental health is to highlight that the diagnosis of mental health conditions is not as scientific as diagnosis for physical medical conditions. In terms of physical health and illnesses, there are often identified patterns of symptoms and clear 'markers' eg: results of a blood test, whilst there are no reliable biological markers for mental health conditions. There are no tests or scans that can show a person 'has' a mental health problem.

Social perspectives on depression follow a similar theme. If a person is in a deeply unsatisfactory relationship, if they are being abused, if they are isolated and/or are in a constant state of grinding poverty is it any surprise they become depressed? Depression is often characterised by low mood, poor motivation, broken sleep patterns (difficulty getting to sleep and difficulty getting up). The person is deeply unhappy. It is not surprising the person has difficulty getting up or difficulty with motivation since they have nothing to look forward to that day.

If some mental health conditions are a response to a person's situation, then the use of medication raises various questions. One of the main points is that the medication will not alter the life difficulties the person is facing and that these life difficulties could be the cause of the person's mental health problems.

By diagnosing a person with, say, depression when the cause of the depression is an abusive relationship or poverty etc, then the individual is being cast into the 'sick' role. Arguably the person is not sick at all. The environment the person is having to live in is 'sick' and so this should be addressed.

Social perspectives on mental health have been further developed by discussions about cultural sensitivity. Many of the 'markers' used by doctors in diagnosis can be viewed in culturally specific ways. So that, for example, what is viewed as an inappropriate response in one culture can be viewed as entirely appropriate in another culture.

Drug and Alcohol Dependency

In drug and alcohol services there has been a debate for many years about whether a medical perspective or a social perspective is more helpful. The social perspective on drug and alcohol dependency would argue that attention needs to be paid to the social and relationship difficulties that a person has experienced that have resulted in them misusing drugs or alcohol.

Addressing the original problems or addressing the service user's perception of the original problems should result in the service user starting to regain a sense of control in their life which will enable them to regain control of their substance use.

The medical perspective would argue that where a person has been consuming significant amounts of drugs or alcohol for five years or so, then a physiological addiction has been established. There has been

such a significant change in the brain that the person has a genuine
physiological craving for the substance if the person stops consuming
it. The compulsion to have a drink or a 'fix' becomes stronger as
more is consumed.

The craving to have drugs or alcohol therefore develops a momentum
of its own. Also, the slide into dependency may, or may not, have
been due to personal and social difficulties. However, the strength of
the addiction creates difficulties because the individual could lose
their job, spend all their finances on drug or alcohol use, and their
social network could collapse about them as they steal money from
family and are absorbed in the need to feed their addiction.

Chaotic drug or alcohol use is characterised by social irresponsibility
since the physiological addiction is so strong. Once a person's drug
or alcohol use has become so chaotic, then the rehabilitation
(abstinence) approach brings together aspects of the social and the
medical model.

Understanding medical and social perspectives and
associated processes is vital. It is also important to
acknowledge that the perspectives are exactly that –
perspectives – not necessarily fact and reality. Just as the
constructionist approach would argue, we would encourage
students to question concepts and perhaps use the "best" of
each approach to support work with service users.

As suggested activities:

➢ list with the student any statements they have heard
   made about individuals by other workers or agencies
   which indicate subscription to social or medical
   perspectives

➢ consider the barriers which people from different
   groups may face in accessing the setting in which the
   student is placed and what the setting does to address
   this.

THE RECOVERY MODEL

6

The recovery movement has developed since the 1990s, although it can trace aspects of its roots back further. The recovery movement is a counter to the view that of all those with long term enduring mental health problems a third would need continual psychiatric care (with a significant death rate through suicide), a third would need intermittent psychiatric care and a third would be able to lead relatively ordinary lives, with support, after a period of poor mental health. The recovery movement points to an increasing body of evidence that 50% to 68% of individuals make a complete or near complete recovery. In a way, the recovery model can be seen as a challenge to both the social and medical model.

The recovery movement has no set conditions but common aspects include the following:

➢ Finding someone who will hold a "candle of hope". People who achieve recovery relate the importance of having people around them who continue to hope and convey a sense of confidence that recovery will eventually occur.

➢ Refusing to be called or referred to by a diagnosis eg: 'schizophrenic'. The individual needs to remind themselves and others that they are a person and not an 'illness'.

➢ Changing one's attitude to conditions. This can include individuals deciding not to 'collaborate' with their label.

➢ Developing attitudes of self reliance, personal responsibility and countering internalised sense of self loathing, shame and fear.

➢ Recognising the strengths and abilities of individuals.

➢ Finding meaning and purpose despite symptoms persisting (e.g.: recovery does not mean an individual will never hear voices again).

➢ Healing from the effects of the stigma and discrimination. Finding ways to return to work or education etc.

➢ Empowerment. The development of a person's sense of control over decision making in their own life is vital to recovery. Professionals need to respect the individual's expertise about their own situation.

➤ Peer support, mentoring and guidance. An effective and supportive social network.

➤ Additional support to those who have experienced trauma and or abuse and for those who have drug or alcohol addictions.

Psychiatrists who support the recovery movement would also place the importance of observing drug treatments in this list. Many service users would as well, although they may place drug treatments within a framework of receiving information about drugs and entering into a discussion with mental health professionals about exactly which drugs are most beneficial for them.

The recovery model is gaining momentum in mental health services. It is increasingly referred to as the personal recovery model in acknowledgement that the whole concept of the model is that 'recovery' is an intensely personal process and that individuals are the experts on their own situation. There is a growing sense that just as the medical and social model perspectives can be applied to a range of service user groups and services, so the recovery model may have merit in other areas.

In mental health services, you will probably have a range of discussion points to use with a student in discussing the recovery model with a student. You could use the bullet points covering the common themes of the recovery model – which of these are relevant/in place for the service user being discussed?

If you work outside of mental health and this theory appeals to you and a student, discuss the model and ask the student what aspects may be applicable to areas of practice other than mental health: particularly your own area.

SOCIAL CONSTRUCTIONISM

7

Like all theories, the heart of social constructionism is quite simple, but it has quickly developed a language that is itself a barrier to understanding.

Social constructionists acknowledge that realities are constructed in a range of ways. The "realities" which health professionals hold may be very different to those of social care professionals. In many ways, this builds on an understanding of the social and medical model.

Social constructionism highlights a basic truth that most societal views are generated by people (social) and then applied through the activity of public services and other organisations (constructed). One of the consequences of this is that views and opinions can change and so the way that society orders itself can also change.

It is probably best to give examples of this. For many years Chris Phillipson has argued that old age is constructed by the capitalist system (e.g.: 1998). In the 1980s when there was high unemployment and it appeared that this would remain, there was talk of retirement starting at age 60 for most people. This was partly so that the unemployment figures could be reduced. However, once the state became aware of the increasing longevity of people's lives and the implications this would have for state funding then the debate turned the opposite way. The state retirement age has been raised to 65 for women (to be the same as men) and it is likely that the state pension age will rise to 68 in the UK within the next 30 years or so.

The age at which someone should retire from work is not "naturally determined". As a society we decide. We will decide as a result of consideration of various factors such as the cost to society (and us!)

Childhood is another concept that is socially constructed. There are still many older people alive today who left school at 14 or 15 and started work. The age of consent for sex was only raised to 16 in the 1880s, but before then it was 14. There are many societies that allow young women to marry at 14 or so. The Netherlands moved the age of consent for sex down to 14 in the 1990s.

In the UK there has been a movement to protect and extend childhood until the young person celebrates their 18th birthday. One example of this is the law relating to abuse of trust. This law makes it an offence for a teacher or care worker to have sexual contact with a 16 or 17 year old they are in day to day contact with through work. The age for the legal purchase of tobacco has recently been raised from 16 to 18. A Bill is currently going through Parliament with the intention of raising the school leaving age to 18.

The social construction of health and social care can also be seen in the way the main ethos and focus of our work has changed. Until the1960s the role of health and social care services that were involved with people with mental health problems, people with learning disabilities and people with physical disabilities was to act as agents of social control.

People with care needs were placed in large institutions. They were congregated together, segregated from society. Society comforted itself by saying "they're best with their own" and "they wouldn't be able to cope in society". Crudely put – care staff were social police. In the 1950s some of the long stay learning disability hospitals had individuals in them who were so independent and so aware of their detention that they escaped. Some evaded recapture.

As a result of various developments the focus of social work has moved from agent of social control to empowerment of service users. What a turn around! This has been as a result of protests from service users (arguably people with physical disabilities have been prominent, but all social care groups have been involved in promoting their rights). Additionally carers have often expressed the rights of their loved ones for a decent, ordinary life. There have also been professionals who have been prominent in wanting services to improve.

Social constructionists would raise various questions, for example "Are we really empowering people or are we better at hiding the fact that we are still agents of social control?" This question is most relevant to mental health services and children's services, but there are times when it applies to all social work services.

It is also particularly relevant when the question of race and ethnicity is added. Mental health services have singularly failed to shake off institutional racism. The number of African Caribbean men who are compulsory detained is disproportionately high compared to white men who are compulsory detained.

There have been significant changes in social care in the last 40 years and things continue to move apace. At present social care and social work are being pulled into other professional areas. For example, children's services are being pulled into education. There are competing pressures – firstly for more individual care, secondly the cost of care is rising, the cost of individualised care is huge. Could this be resolved by community involvement? Technology and robotics? Could the role of a social worker be reserved for the most vulnerable (reinforcing the sense of stigma associated with having a social worker)? Will the articulate middle classes arrange social care services for themselves or their loved ones in the same way they book a package holiday on the internet? Self assessment is already being promoted. In effect, people who self assess can refer themselves on to the key professional (e.g.: occupational therapist) without the need for a social worker. However social work looks now, practitioners need to recognise that their field is not a fixed notion in itself and will change in the years ahead.

Students entering the profession will be at different stages in understanding their own place within this constructed reality and it may be challenging for them to reflect on these issues in supervision. Students are also in a unique position whilst on placement in being able to reflect upon their own agency's role as creator, sustainer and challenger of views and norms of that service's users and their issues.

<u>Language</u>

The social constructionist perspective emphasises that language is a major tool. Beckett (2006) points out that much social work and social care activity focuses on problems, needs and risks. There is an air of negativity and burden about the way service users are discussed.

The pressure for social care and social work staff to be negative about service users has increased in recent years. Eligibility criteria (the threshold which must be reached before services are agreed) have been introduced (and raised higher) resulting in staff emphasising how difficult the behaviour of a person is or how significant a person's care needs are etc, in order to access resources. It is important to enable students to analyse when other workers may take this stance and why.

There are links between language and social imagery and the way that language can be dehumanising. This theme is central to social constructionism. One clear example is the way that the language used to describe key needs can be dehumanising. For example, regular reference is made to service users needing "feeding" or within assessment and care planning documentation questions are asked about "feeding". Feeding is a word we generally use in conjunction with animals (feeding time at the zoo) or babies. Most adults "eat". They do not "feed themselves". However, in relation to people in receipt of social and health care, language changes – people are dehumanised and effectively negative social roles are constructed.

Self Narrative/Self Perception

Social constructionists also emphasise the importance of self narrative. The person with mental health problems who stops taking medication can be viewed by professionals as not complying with their care plan. The service user's view may be that the medication has pervasive side effects that reduces their quality of life. Children's services are increasingly open to how teenagers view their experience of being "looked after". However, both these examples illustrate that there are limitations. If the mental health service user stops taking their medication and then commits suicide, or the teenager wants to stay out till all hours both may be seen as at significant risk. After a point, services have to be pragmatic, regardless of the theoretical perspective.

There are situations where a social constructionist perspective could be applied but isn't. An example could be the older person who quietly but clearly says they want to remain in their own home even if they hardly move from their chair for risk of falling. Still social workers can listen to the son or daughter express their anxiety and then see the older person forced into attending a day centre or even entering residential care.

It is an old saying that in history the winners write the history books. In social care and social work, we need to avoid the situation where the assessment is entirely the viewpoint of the assessor. In social work we must avoid the person being described solely by family

members and professionals. The service user's perspective must be
acknowledged. It is to be seen if it can then be acted on.

Often concepts of constructionism are presented very
academically and workers and students likewise struggle to see
how this theory may apply to their everyday work. However,
there are potentially a number of basic but useful applications.
For example, supervision could support students to self assess
how they:

➢ Use anti-oppressive language which promotes dignity and
respect

➢ Question "reality". When presented with a problem/issue
etc. staff shouldn't necessarily accept this as fact. Whose
reality is this? How is the problem defined or constructed?

➢ Where a person tells you they "should" do something,
question why? People should not feel under pressure from
social norms, as this can lead to a curtailment of choices.

➢ Encourage people to express their feelings and adopt a
"narrative" approach

➢ Listen to service users and carers.

In addition, we would suggest it can be helpful to spend some
time with the student assessing how the placement setting
itself is a socially constructed "reality", and what function the
service serves. This is applied constructionism (see chapter 2).

SOCIAL ROLE VALORISATION   (8)

Social role valorisation (previously known as normalisation), is a development of the principle of normalisation first expressed in Scandinavian countries in the late 1960s. One of the main writers who has helped to develop Social Role Valorisation is Wolf Wolfensberger (1983). See also Wolfensberger and Thomas (1983).

Social role valorisation/normalisation began in learning disabilities services. However, in recent years, it has been more widely applied and is now seen as applicable throughout social work.

There are seven themes to the principle of Social Role Valorisation (SRV). If you think of SRV as a parent with seven children, all of whom do and say different things but together make up a family, this gives us an idea of the way in which the seven themes work together.

SRV is made up of language which on the face of it is jargonistic and difficult to understand. However, once we look beneath the jargon it is very easy to see how the principle of SRV and the seven core themes relate to social work practice. Whatever you do, don't let the language put you off – work through each of the core themes and look at applying them to your day to day work.

1.   The Role of (Un)Consciousness in Human Services

For us to begin to look at what this first theme means in practice, carry out the following exercise with a student (or group of students):

Think back to your childhood and try to identify the first time you came into contact with someone who had either a physical disability or a learning disability. It may be that you have *always* known a person with a disability (for example a family member) so in this case think back to your earliest memories of them. Alternatively, you may remember isolated examples such as seeing a person using a wheelchair when you were out etc. Whatever the situation was, think about how you felt and what you did at the time. Remember this is about when you were a child, no one is going to judge or assess you on the feelings you had then or on what you did. You must be as honest as possible for us to look at this theme effectively.

What you might find, as you reflect back, is that one of the feelings you had was curiosity. Children are often curious about people with disabilities. As a result of this curiosity they ask questions, of the person themselves, their parents, a teacher etc. If you have contact with children yourself you may have heard the kinds of questions – *"Why does that man walk like that?" "Why does she look like that?"* etc. The problem comes when adults don't give reasonable answers to these questions. Children might be told *"Shush – stop looking. I told you not to stare"* or *"He's very poorly"* or *"She's no different to you or me".* Of course these answers are the start of some of the other feelings you might have identified – if you were told as a child that someone was "poorly" – you might feel sorry for them (pity); on the other hand if you were rushed away and told not to look you might have begun to feel afraid.

This is basically the process of socialisation. Our early experiences often form our values and feelings and very often these are negative. If we are honest, we will have a mixture of feelings towards the people we work with and these may change over time, or in terms of context. These current feelings may not always be respectful and positive and some of them may be influenced by our earlier experiences.

What this theme is saying is that both individuals and society in general, carry negative feelings towards people who need care services. These are usually unconscious and can be formed throughout our socialisation. Since human services are staffed by individuals and form part of society, these feelings can be expressed through service delivery. It is a stated aim of SRV to be honest about unconscious thoughts and processes within services, so that they can be directly addressed.

This theme carries one of Wolfensberger's brilliant insights. Society values some qualities (eg. young adult, attractive, wealthy etc) as positive and views some qualities as negative (ageing, physical disability, learning disability etc). In relation to the qualities society views negatively it feels it cannot be honest and explicitly negative. So society's negative view goes into the societal 'unconscious'. Society masks its dislike of people who are different by creating services that are meant to 'care' for the people who are viewed negatively. But these 'care services' have an unspoken (and primary) goal of keeping people viewed as different and deviant away from mainstream (valued) society. The explicit goal of care services (to help service users) is only their secondary goal. Since society considers the people in the services to be unimportant the services are poorly resourced. Hence the quality of care is at risk of being poor. Therefore Wolfensberger's brilliant insight was that traditional care services are part of the oppressive structure that service users face. Services need to be honest about their origins and the need for them to change before they can adequately support service users to become valued members of society. This is very linked to ideas of social constructionism.

2. Role Expectancy and Role Circularity

This theme is very closely related to the processes of stereotyping and labelling. It is basically what is often known as the self-fulfilling prophecy.

The idea is that individuals who are already valued will have positive experiences and high expectations will be placed on them, which they will strive to fulfill. Individuals who are at risk of devaluation will have fewer demands placed on them, and expectations will be low and stereotyped. There will therefore be little motivation, or encouragement, to excel or reach their potential. For example, people could be denied opportunities because they are not expected to benefit.

3. The Conservatism Corollary

Of all the language used in terms of the seven core themes this is probably the most jargonistic. It is nothing to do with party politics.

This theme is also informally known as the positive option. Essentially it states that people who are at risk of devaluation will be further devalued unless the *most* valued social role/activity/relationship is offered and experienced. As services, we often fail to seek the most valued life experiences for people. We should always strive to use the most positive images and activities in service delivery to enhance the status of service users.

4. The Developmental Model/Personal Competency Enhancement

We all continue to learn and develop throughout our adult lives. No one could say that their learning ended when they left school. This theme basically states that there must be an assumption on the part of services that through the use of social education, positive experiences, facilitation of learning, high expectations etc. all individuals can experience tremendous growth.

One of the failings of services in relation to this area is linked closely to role expectancy and role circularity. If individuals are not expected to learn it is unlikely that they will.

One of the best known messages from this theme is what has become known as age appropriateness. This theme would assert that adults are unlikely to learn when taught as though they were children. We only need to compare teaching in schools to that in colleges of adult education to see the differences between the ways in which children and adults are taught.

5.   The Power of Imitation

Imitation is one of the most powerful learning mechanisms known – in terms of adult learning, imitation is often referred to as 'modelling'. Often people will pick up the mannerisms of their family/partner because they are living together and begin to mimic each other. A more formal example would be the way in which students and new workers 'imitate' or model their behaviour on more experienced colleagues.

This theme of SRV states that positive role modelling should be capitalised on by services for the benefit of service users. It is very closely related to social learning theory.

6.   The Dynamics and Relevance of Social Imagery

Social imagery is really about the portrayal of people who are often devalued by society. It relates to a range of areas, such as:

➢   media

➢   use of language

➢   pictures, posters, décor

➢   names of services

➢   use of names for people in receipt of services

Services should strive to promote positive social imagery and challenge negative imagery. As one of the main mechanisms of oppression, social imagery feeds into the processes of stereotyping and labelling.

7. The Importance of Personal Social Integration and Valued Social Participation

Basically, this is referring to the segregation which people in receipt of social care can face. This theme states that services should seek to counter this segregation of individuals and groups. However, social integration must work alongside social participation. Since the run down of the old institutions (eg. hospitals for people with learning disabilities and psychiatric hospitals), some of the services which have replaced them have largely become mini-institutions in the community.

It is vital that as well as living in the community, people take part in their local community. Where people are only physically integrated and not *personally* integrated lip service is being paid to SRV.

Service Accomplishments

Service development in response to SRV has been variable. Unfortunately various professionals have not always understood some of the main points made by SRV. In fairness Wolfensberger's description of SRV can be complex.

Partly in response to this other writers have sought to explain options for service development in more accessible ways. One example is O'Brien's service accomplishments (O'Brien 1980). Originally there were five but these have been increased. Often people now talk of the seven accomplishments. These are:-

Status and respect: Each person should receive a service that enhances their sense of self-esteem.

Choice: Everyone should be offered choices and supported to make choices relating to day to day and major life decisions.

Competence: Everyone should be supported to learn and develop across a whole range of areas.

Community presence: Everyone should be in ordinary communities; accessing services and facilities in the same way as other members of the community.

Relationships: Everyone should have a network of relationships which include a partner, family and friends.

Individuality: The uniqueness of each individual and the need for individual self expression must be recognised.

Continuity: Each individual should experience a natural progression in their life. When change in one part of a person's life occurs care must be taken to minimise disruption in all other parts of the person's life.

Consider an assessment with the student and analyse how the principles of SRV might influence the assessment and subsequent planning.

Consider each of the 7 service accomplishments – how has the student included the principles? What does the theory add to their way of approaching planning in the future?

DISCOURSE ANALYSIS

Discourse analysis (or critical analysis) is a way of questioning that seeks to identify the assumptions that social relations are based on.

Discourse analysis has been used in many disciplines. Traditionally, one of the main uses has been in the field of linguistics, where discourse analysis has been used to analyse language and text. It is an approach that studies the organisation of language not in grammatical terms so much, as the broader source, use or intention of language. The social context of the language and the interaction that is generated are important parts of the whole analysis.

In the social sciences, discourse analysis has been used to deconstruct the use of language. Since everything has to be described in some way (language or text is used), then this means that everything can be deconstructed by the use of discourse analysis.

Arguably, discourse analysis is a very academic activity. Within some of the disciplines that use discourse analysis, the language used is very esoteric (understandable only to an 'in' club of people).

All Social Structures and Relations are Socially Created

The rise of discourse analysis is partly due to the ending of the view that there is some established ordering or meaning in the human world. Post modernism has the view that all societies and all relationships are socially constructed (humans, in some ways, decide how they wish to arrange society).

The ordering of society is not based on a 'natural' structure or universal truth. Once people have created a social system, this then becomes rooted and established. Its legitimacy is asserted through various claims (language). All these claims can be analysed and questioned. The motivations of people (others and ourselves) should be identifiable through discourse analysis. One of the assumptions of discourse analysis is that all social perceptions are subjective and that dominant social perceptions (or beliefs) are just expressions of the dominant discourses that are able to exert influence or control over society at that time. There is no intrinsic, absolute truth.

Discourse analysis is not intended to establish a new answer. It is seeking to reveal the underlying assumptions, motives and politics that are located within and around language, text and social relations.

Discourse Analysis and Politics

Some of the very fertile fields for discourse analysis (although it is now used in numerous fields) are those of politics, social policy and ideology. These fields are profoundly dependent on language and text and so open themselves to an analysis of their discourses (discussions, claims or arguments).

One example is the contribution of elite racism to institutional racism in Western Europe. Discourse analysis has been used to explain how elites are able to maintain dominant discourses through the media, political propaganda, business policies, advertising etc. Parliamentary debates focus on "illegal" immigration (these concepts could be broken down themselves by discourse analysis). The dominant discourses focus on claims of the problems immigrants create, the threat to 'our' culture and the cost to 'us'. The dominant discourse focuses on the alleged harm done to us and fails to make any acknowledgement of the problems experienced by immigrants caused by institutions in the UK. The pervasiveness of the dominant discourse can be expressed by discourse analysis. Additionally, the limited in-roads that anti-racist discourses have made compared to very recent anti-terrorist discourses which subtly (and not so subtly) re-enforce racist discourses, illustrates the dominance of elitist discourses.

Discourse analysis, at its most helpful, can aid in the breaking down of cultural assumptions and make clear the societal power biases that oppress minorities. At its most esoteric, some of the language is almost impenetrable and is mainly of use to academics.

Approaching this with a student would be closely linked to their practice setting. Some examples could be:

➢ Analysis of the idealisation of the rural v community isolation and resource deficits in services which cover urban and rural settings

➢ The idealisation of mythical "childhood" v the demonisation of young people in our culture in a YOT setting

➢ Local assumptions about cultural difference specific to the context and location of a service

There is no one Feminist Theory! Rather there has been development of a range of perspectives and points which have been loosely grouped together. These perspectives have shared values which include:

> a recognition of the extensive inequalities in society based on gender with men consistently being dominant

> the need to be woman focused and the recognition that a glib gender blind approach won't work

> it isn't just a case of promoting more women into management posts. The sources of power and the construction of hierarchies should be questioned themselves

> related to this is the social construction of male dominance, especially in the use of language but also in gender roles more broadly

> a recognition of the diversity of women's experience. The experience of black women, disabled women and gay women has been different from white heterosexual women

The Impact of Feminist Arguments

Given the variety of feminist viewpoints it is possibly helpful to point out some of the success of the feminist movement.

> Feminism has successfully highlighted the extensiveness of domestic violence and has campaigned for violence on women partners to be seen in the same way as violence in the street on a stranger. Amazingly, until the mid 1990s a husband could not be accused of raping his wife even though rape in marriage in the UK was a daily occurrence.

The development of the women's aid movement and refuges has been a key aspect of liberating women from violent oppression.

> The power of language and the importance of using inclusive language has been promoted by feminists (and others involved in anti-oppressive practice). Although there is a sense that this

achievement is vulnerable (and it has certainly been extensively trivialised and mocked), it has resulted in the development of language that is far more inclusive.

➤ There has been a recognition that societal developments and social policy initiatives affect men and women differently (because of their gender) and this has been challenged. The role of women as unpaid carers of (adult) family members with personal care needs is one example. Community care initiatives (social policy) have focused on enabling adults with personal care needs to stay at home. This has meant that there are pressures on women carers to carry on in their (unpaid) role.

In children's services the pressure on women is two-fold. Firstly the societal pressure to be competent mothers and then the social pressure to move off benefits and return to work as soon as possible after having children.

The feminist perspective has promoted various responses. Firstly, work with women is women centred. There is an explicit desire for the working relationship to empower the woman carer, parent or service user. As Dominelli (2002) has written *"The assessment process is likely to involve redefining the problem being considered from a feminist perspective. This removes it from the private realm of a personal problem for which the woman is solely responsible and lodges it in the public domain as a social problem which she is experiencing individually along with a number of other women".*

Secondly, feminist social care and social work has promoted the need for women only space. This has implications for all services. In health services the use of mixed wards has raised a range of concerns. At a fundamental level is the physical safety of women in-patients. The importance of single gender wards has been emphasised for some years. Women only groups in mental health services and learning disability services are known to be empowering. Women only groups in leaving care services are also considered to enhance the self esteem and confidence of young women.

Thirdly, the feminist perspective has called for social policy initiatives to provide equality of opportunity through the provision of adequate child care and, in adult services, a range of service options that will give carers a real choice.

Continuing Development

Although the feminist perspective has initiated some significant developments there are areas that it continues to grapple with. There are practical aspects and theoretical aspects.

In terms of practical considerations one of the feminist perspective's goals is still not fully attained. The continuing level of domestic violence and the lack of a comprehensive, co-ordinated response that provides effective support for women and children and challenges violent men can leave women fearful about approaching professional agencies (Mullender 2002).

The feminist perspective has noticeably failed to adequately address structural inequalities within social care and social work organisations. In employment terms some 75% of the workforce in social care organisations are women. The proportion of men in senior management has remained stubbornly high and has only recently dropped below 75% of all senior managers.

In terms of continuing debates Orme (2002) has identified:-

1) The continuing uncertainty about whether women should be seen as different from men. How far should feminist perspectives argue that women have qualities that are different to men? This could cut across arguments for equal opportunities and could result in reinforcing gendered roles (e.g.: women are better at caring than men).

2) The feminist perspective has criticised social work for failing to recognise the power relationship and power imbalance between the woman professional and the woman service user. The woman professional is applying laws and policies that are discriminatory against women. Women need to influence the policy debates at a National level as well as work at the level of the individual. This individual aspect includes acknowledging diversity and the power that exists in all relationships.

3) The way that feminist perspectives should seek to engage men has been contested. Some feminists would argue that this detracts from what should be the central focus, identifying the discrimination that women face and working with women to counter this. Other feminists feel there needs to be engagement

with men to address the levels of violence and inequality women experience from men and to call men to take responsibility for the way they develop their masculinity and to exercise the power they have in collaboration and dialogue with women.

The feminist perspective is an active illustration of the constructionist position. Society is socially constructed. If we want to, we can restructure society. However, the partial successes of the feminist movement also illustrate that the dominant power elites are quite satisfied with how society is structured. Whilst some ground has been conceded (or won by women), most of the land remains in the ownership of the same elite.

Discuss the following questions with a student in supervision.

➤ To what extent might the feminist perspective critique agency policy and practice?

➤ Can a male worker make use of feminist perspectives? If so, how?

➤ Can a feminist perspective influence work with just women service users?

BLACK PERSPECTIVES

Black perspectives have been developed by many different academics, practitioners and service users. There are a number of themes and elements some of which are located within a theoretical framework, whilst other elements are more applied.

<u>Racism and White Ideology</u>

The black perspective has made clear that racism is based on White European/White North American ideological beliefs about the claimed superiority of white people over non-white people. This white ideology has been used to justify the enslavement of Africans from the early 17th Century onwards as well as the colonisation and control of Africa and other parts of the world from the 16th Century onwards.

At various times, the white ideology has invoked nature and God for its justification. It has also become self re-inforcing. British history and the manner in which Britain applied white ideology (slave trade and colonisation) leaves a residual white arrogance.

Other non white cultures have recognised differences but they have not developed the involved ideological claims of superiority. In this sense, racism is a white construction.

<u>White Eurocentric Theory</u>

It is against this backdrop of unconscious white views of superiority that all the significant psychological theories and social work theories have been developed. White European culture has progressively championed the individual since the end of the Middle Ages. The rights of the individual and the importance of autonomy and self reliance have been key white themes since John Locke wrote in the late 1600s.

By contrast, many other cultures of the world have focused on the importance of achieving fulfillment by engagement and integration within a community. Mutuality, interdependence and spiritual connections are some of the goals that individuals within other cultures may strive for.

The inherent cultural biases within theories need to be recognised. Counselling approaches are deeply embedded in a white, Eurocentric, individualistic approach. Attachment theory has been used to validate the Eurocentric nuclear family and so implicitly denigrate alternative family structures and social arrangements relating to the care and nurture of children.

Within English social work, the practice of community social work has virtually died. English social work is focused on individual case management which, arguably, consists of little more than bureaucratic procedures.

Community social work is relevant for communities that face structural barriers and institutional discrimination. Black communities that experience economic and social disadvantage are more likely to benefit from community social work aimed at education, awareness raising and empowerment. However, the triumph of individualistic social work case management disproportionately affects black communities compared to white communities (since poverty, unemployment, poor housing and poor educational opportunities disproportionately affect black people in Britain).

Feminist perspectives have been dominated by white women writers. In America, black women writers have formulated the concept of womanism. Womanism differs from feminism in that a woman comes to value herself as a woman in whatever role she may choose for herself. Within white feminism is the expectation that the woman will commit herself to meaningful action towards feminist goals. The womanist concept supports the development of a flexible, personal, positive self identity of what it means to be a woman (Ossana et al 1992).

More generally, many theories are based on an assumption of 'normality' as defined within White European or White North American culture. The more an individual, group or community from a non-white culture deviate from this 'normal' ideal, the increased likelihood that the individual or group will be pathologised. Arguably, it is within mental health services and children's services that this effect is most noticeable. The extent of institutional racism within mental health services has been a continuing problem (eg: see National Institute for Mental Health in England 2003). The exact reasons for the institutional racism are not clear. Factors such as aversive experiences in society (e.g.: racism) and structural inequalities also play a part. However, cultural views of what is 'normal' and therefore what is abnormal are likely to contribute.

In children's services there is evidence of over representation of African children and children of dual heritage in the looked after system. Also, there is evidence that family centres are not equally accessible and black families do not get support that is available to white families (Dutt and Phillips 2000). Again, there are likely to be various factors that contribute to this of which an unconscious white racism towards black families is only one element.

Development of Black Identity

Within social care and social work there has been much debate about supporting positive identity formation. Often this debate has been held in children's services but it can equally apply to adult services.

One of the most influential theories of black identity formation is that of William Cross (1971, 1980 and 1991). The theory is termed Nigrescence, which means the process of becoming black in a white society. Cross identified that there are five stages that a black person will go through. These are:

1. Pre-encounter. The black person will identify with white people and white culture. The black person will be negative towards black people and could engage in self loathing. This is basically a process of internalisation of racism.

2. Encounter. The person has an experience or a number of experiences that are unnerving. Examples include the person experiencing racism from white people. As a result of this, the person feels anxious and insecure. They start on a journey of questioning and self examination.

3. Immersion-Emmersion. The person 'immerses' themselves into black culture. They may change their style of dress, diet, friendships etc. There are aspects to the immersion stage that indicate the person lacks control, partly due to a reaction against their experience in the Encounter stage. However, the Emmersion process represents a process of regaining control, often by identifying with black role models.

4.   Internalisation. The person becomes secure in their black
     identity. This often results in a decline in the persons anti-white
     sentiment but a continuing sense of anger at racism. The person
     is usually able to mix socially with white people but their principle
     social network is with black people.

5.   Internalisation-commitment. The person has the ability to
     recognise the importance of countering all discrimination and is
     able to live out a concern for society as a whole. This stage is
     often associated with older adults.

Nigrescence theory could be useful for staff in children's services who
are working with black adolescents. However, staff need to avoid
using this (and any theory) in a blanket manner. This ties in with one
of the themes of black perspectives – that there is diversity within
black communities. A blanket application of any one anti-racist
approach by services will be only partially effective.

Additionally some anti-racist practices are applied half heartedly.
Owusu-Bempah (2002) is critical of racial identity and self concept
programmes for black children who are looked after. Such
programmes often focus on the individual child and ignore the
broader structural reasons why the child entered the care system.

Elements of Black Perspectives

Any list of elements or aspects of black perspectives is going to be
partial and incomplete. The development of black perspectives is one
of the most dynamic debates in social work. That said however, black
perspectives include:

➤   A celebration of diversity. This includes recognising diversity
     between individuals, how families are structured, community
     relationships. Cultural diversity, language and history are to be
     enjoyed.

➤   Valuing the contribution of black people and the intellectual
     insights of black writers. Cross' theory of identity development is
     potentially relevant to all people who go through a process of
     personal liberation (women, gay men and gay women etc.).

➤   Recognition of the strengths of black people and communities.
     Many black voluntary organisations have started with little or no
     state support. There is an increasing range of services that seek

to support people from minority communities in culturally appropriate ways.

➤ Exposing the extensiveness of racism and highlighting the oppressive effects it has.

➤ Articulating the need for anti-racist practice to be dynamic and flexible, able to address the different forms that racism adopts (e.g.: institutional, unconscious etc.)

➤ Challenging White Eurocentric/White North American attitudes, beliefs, structures and systems.

➤ A commitment to equality and rights. Through the application of anti-racist practice other oppressive practices will be exposed and challenged.

<u>Implications for Practice</u>

Social workers and students need to be honest about the extensiveness and destructiveness of racism and the unconscious ways that white Eurocentric beliefs and practices are considered superior to non white beliefs and practices.

Students need to avoid applying a blanket approach to their work with black people in which they prejudge the person and assume a certain text book, anti-racism strategy should be applied. Maybe that particular strategy is going to be beneficial but it should not be assumed. Rather, it is important to engage with an individual and the broader community and to understand the person through their own words and their expression of their own identity.

As a practice assessor, it is vital to cultivate the student's own potential for learning and the development of your own and their anti-oppressive practice. Make clear you are open to being challenged.

In supervision discussion with student, raise the following questions:

➢ In what ways might black perspectives critique agency policy and practice?

➢ Should black perspectives influence only work with black service users?

➢ How might the student be able to draw on black perspectives in their ongoing practice?

➢ How might black perspectives critique some of theories covered in other sections of this book?

C MODELS FOR UNDERSTANDING PEOPLES SITUATIONS: HUMAN DEVELOPMENT AND LEARNING

Students need a thorough understanding of theories around human development in order to be able to understand and assess the service user's world. This relates to settings with young people and adults as the impact of early experiences can be life-long, and people's development is ongoing through life. The need for students to undertake specific learning and assessment around human development is referred to in the *Requirements for Social Work Training* (DoH 2002:3).

Linked to this, students need understanding of how people learn. This is again a theoretical basis to help understand people, but also one which should inform processes and interventions which aim at supporting peoples' learning and change.

Practice assessors require a sound basis in all of these concepts in order to support the student's own learning on placement. Think of it as a dual process where modelling self directed learning as an adult will enable students to put this into practice in their own interactions with service users, colleagues and other professionals.

The topics covered in this section are:

➢ Child development
➢ Adult development
➢ Grief and loss
➢ Attachment
➢ Learning theories
➢ Attribution theory

FURTHER READING

Crawford, K. and Walker, J. (2007) *Social Work and Human Development.* (Exeter) Learning Matters.

Jarvis, P. (2003) *Adult Education and Lifelong Learning: Theory and Practice.* (Oxon) Routledge.

Lindon, J. (2005) *Understanding Child Development Linking Theory and Practice.* (London) Hodder Arnold.

Mezirow, J. and Associates (2000) *Learning as Transformation: Critical perspectives on a Theory in Progress.* (San Francisco) Jossey Bass.

Newman, B. and Newman, P. (2007) *Theories of Human Development.* (Oxon) Routledge.

Rayner, E., Clulow, C., Twyman. M. and Rose, J. (2005) *Human Development.* (London) Psychology Press.

Robinson, L. (2007) *Cross-Cultural Child Development for Social Workers: An Introduction.* (Basingstoke) Palgrave MacMillan.

CHILD DEVELOPMENT (12)

There are various theories and models of child development. Some of these focus on the child's intellectual development whilst others seek to embrace the social and emotional development of a child.

Most of the models have one thing in common. They consider that there are definable stages that the vast majority of children go through, which are driven by the biological and physical development of the child.

Erikson

Erik Erikson (1950) developed a model of human development titled the "Eight Ages of Man". Erikson described each stage as a struggle between two emotional opposites. The first stage is characterised by the emotions trust and mistrust. The child's experience would result in the child adopting one of these emotions as a dominant (unconscious) outlook. If the child came through the first stage trusting people, there is still a chance that future negative experiences could result in the child losing trust in those around them.

The five stages of the eight stages identified by Erikson that relate to children are:

Stage One: Trust – Mistrust. Age 0 to 1 year. The child will feel able to trust the world and people in the world if their needs are responded to and the child is cared for. Emotional warmth and a sense of belonging from adult caregivers are crucial to building up a sense of trust.

Inadequate and rejecting care from adults will result in the child being suspicious and fearful of adults and others.

Stage Two: Antonomy – Doubt. Age 1 to 3 years. Erikson argues that this is the first opportunity the child has to develop a range of life skills. Encouraging this is key to building up the child's confidence. If the child is not positively supported to develop their own skills, or is mocked or criticised when they do learn new skills then the child will be riddled with doubt and lack confidence.

Stage Three: Initiative – Inadequacy (or guilt). Age 3 to 6 years. The child has already got control over their body and their life skills are being increased. In stage three, the child feels able to initiate actions, both physical and verbal. Children who are supported to initiate physical activities, such a bike riding, swimming etc will have their sense of initiative reinforced. Emotional and intellectual initiative will be reinforced by the child's questions being answered whilst conversation and play are encouraged.

If the child's initiative is not encouraged the child will develop a sense of guilt or inadequacy over self initiated activities.

Stage Four: Industry – Inferiority. Age 6 to 12 years. The child has a strong interest in matters of detail. How things work, why events happen, how things are made are all key questions and points of interest for the child.

Children will need to be encouraged in their activities of making, sewing and baking. The end products need to be praised. It is in this sense that the child is industrious. However, if the child's making activities are dismissed as "making a mess" then this can instil a sense of inferiority in the child.

This is also the first stage where the child is aware of other children. The child's sense of industry or inferiority can be shaped by their relative achievements in respect of their peers.

Stage Five: Identity – Role Confusion. Age 12 to 18 years. The child is developing into an adolescent. There are significant biological changes resulting in new feelings and sensations. The adolescent is also increasingly aware of the importance of what other people may think of them. Intellectually, the adolescent is also able to generate ideal images (of family, friendships and society) and contrast them with the imperfections they experience on a daily basis.

Erikson highlighted the importance of identity formation. For the adolescent this is drawn from their family, their own interests and activities, their peers and their aspirations for the future. If the adolescent has had positive experiences in the first four stages of their life, this should result in a higher probability that they will develop a positive identity.

However, such a positive outcome is not guaranteed and a variety of factors could result in the adolescent experiencing role confusion. It was Erikson who introduced the term identity crisis. This role confusion or identity crisis could be generated by:

> the adolescent being unfavourably compared to others

> the adolescent having an interest that their family look down on

> societal expectations eg. Not "fitting in" to certain expectations such as young women are slim, young men will earn lots of money etc.

For some young people, a negative identity is applied to them by others (parents or teachers etc). There is a risk that this informal labelling will result in a self fulfilling prophecy (the adolescent who is labelled 'lazy' by a teacher then does not do their work etc).

Piaget

Jean Piaget developed his stage theory of intellectual development from the 1920s onwards (For example Piaget, 1928.)

Piaget identified four stages. A child moves from one stage to the next as a result of various factors that aid development. These factors are:

> Maturation; this is the physical and cognitive growth that occurs as the child grows up.
> Experience; this is acquired by the child as they engage with the physical world around them.
> Social interaction; the child engages with other people. Piaget was particularly aware of the influences of other (often older) children.
> Equilibration is the way the child draws the first three factors together to establish logic and consistency.

The four stages of development Piaget identified are:

> First stage: Sensorimotor stage. Aged 0 to 2 years. The child uses their senses to actively explore their world. The child becomes aware of their separateness from the world around them. Towards the end of this stage, the child is starting to experiment with objects to see how they fall or move etc.

> Second stage: Preoperational stage. Aged 2 to 6 years. During this stage, the child is egocentric. They are very focussed on their own perspective. Early on in this stage when children play together, it can be as if the children each play their own game, even though they could be side by side.

The child has a view of the world that is objective. Rules are absolute. During this stage, the child grasps the difference in gender and gender roles.

> Third stage: Concrete operational. Aged 7 to 12 years. The child begins to develop their own logic and can organise thoughts in a consistent framework.

Abstract reasoning is still too difficult but physical objects and mathematical problems can be worked on (adding, subtracting and multiplication etc).

The egocentric outlook comes to an end in Stage 3.

> Fourth stage: Formal operations. Aged 11 to 15 years. The young person is able to grasp hypothetical ideas and abstract thinking. The young person can test out theories or hypotheses. Abstract thinking can extend to algebraic mathematics. This stage continues into adulthood.

Vygotsky

In contrast to Piaget's account of cognitive development Lev Vygotsky (1934) wrote about child and adult development in the 1930s and focussed on the impact of culture and society. Vygotsky argued that biological development was significant until the age of 2 or so. After that, although biological development continued this was secondary to the impact of culture, which Vygotsky claims is far more significant. As an illustration Vygotsky points out that biologically speaking humans across the world are very similar. However, there is a huge diversity in how people live and this cannot be explained in terms of biology. It is culture that has generated and then sustains this diversity.

Another of Vygotsky's points is that so much human development is shaped by language (eg. memory, emotions, reasoning, personality, relationships etc). All language is socially constructed.

Vygotsky's approach is complex and difficult to condense. His key point (the importance of culture in generating and shaping child development) is worth hanging on to.

Nature/nurture debate

The perspectives on child development which we have outlined are also key aspects of the nature/nurture debate. The main outline of each camp is:

Nature: Human development is largely a biological process that occurs automatically and follows common (shared) stages. Much of our character, intelligence and our physique/looks is determined by our genes. We will be the way we will be! Nothing can change this.

Nurture: At first, biological development is significant. However, by the time the child is about one, then social relationships and cultural customs will start to profoundly influence the child's personality. Intelligence is not set, it will be markedly enhanced by a stimulating environment (or stunted by a barren care environment).

Sexuality and gender are also not biologically rigid. Gender roles are culturally decided (eg: men work in heavy industry, women look after the family home). Even sexual orientation is malleable. In ancient Greece, among the aristocracy and in the army, male homosexuality was the preferred sexual orientation. Aristocratic men in Greece married women to continue the family line.

Both sides in the nature/nurture debate look at families where behaviour patterns are repeated by one generation to the next. Where a parent develops mental health problems and then a son or daughter develops mental health problems, is this genetic or is the son or daughter (unconsciously) modelling the behaviour of their parents? The son or daughter has a 'green light' to exhibit the same type of behaviours their parents have.

In supervision discussion ask the student about how they might draw on and apply theories of child development in their work.

➤ How do theories of staged development support the student in understanding where individuals are at and what the next stages are?
➤ How might anti-oppressive perspectives (and the theories covered in section A) critique theories of child development?
➤ What influence do perceptions of "the norm" have on how individuals are viewed and how they view themselves?

ADULT DEVELOPMENT (13)

Adult development is a general term that recognises that most adults go through various changes in their life. Each change presents the person with opportunities and potential problems. How the person adjusts to the changes is influenced by the significance of any change, the person's personality and character, their support networks and resources and so on.

Adult development has increasingly emphasised the diversity that exists and that we must not assume that all individuals will progress along one set route.

Child development is characterised by identifiable stages that the vast majority of children will progress through. This includes biological development (their bodies) as well as educational development or development of intelligence, language, moral development etc. When it comes to adult development, there is less agreement as to whether it is helpful to talk of stages.

Erik Erikson (1950) argued that there are identifiable stages in adult development. He stated there are Eight Ages of human development, five of which relate to children, three to adults.

Erikson claimed that each stage was a struggle between two competing emotional and personality based characteristics. The first five stages are reviewed in chapter 12. The three stages that relate to adults are:

➤ Stage Six: Intimacy versus isolation. The person is aged 18 to about 40. In this stage, the adult seeks to establish close meaningful relationships. The relationships do not have to be sexual at all; the important aspect is that there is a mutual emotional bond. If the adult does not establish relationships that have this closeness, the person will have a sense of isolation.

➤ Stage Seven: Generativity versus self absorption. Middle age. In this stage the person will show an interest in the world beyond their immediate family. They will be motivated by a concern for society, the environment and future generations. If a person does not cultivate this outlook, they will become self absorbed and primarily concerned for their own material or hedonistic pursuits.

> Stage Eight: Integrity versus despair. The person is aged about 60 years old or more. The person has time for reflection and as they look back on their life, they may have a sense of satisfaction; this will lead to a feeling of integrity. If the person's reflection results in them feeling they missed key opportunities, then there is an increased risk of experiencing despair. This is partly generated by the sense that it is too late to change anything.

Other writers on adult development are not so committed to the stages model. Even Erikson recognised that the Generativity stage was not tied to middle aged people. Teenagers can show a concern for the world, it's not just middle aged people who want to save the planet!

Hence, many writers on adult development do not promote a stages model. Whilst writers recognise that biological changes do occur (especially the menopause and the process of ageing), many writers argue that outside of these biological changes there is no clear pattern to adult development.

For adults, biological changes are just one factor shaping their life. There are lots of other factors or influences that can have a greater effect on them. Adults do not go through similar emotional and psychological stages at the same time or at similar rates. Some people become wiser as they grow older, some people don't. Physically, one of the main age related factors is the decline in vision, hearing and information processing as we get older.

There does appear to be a historical or generational effect on human development. The people who lived through the Second World War may have a different view to consumption, spending and waste compared to people who have lived through the 1990s. Even if there are generational effects, it still needs to be noted that there are differences within a generation (not all people who were young adults in the 1990s spend and throw away).

Human development models have also emphasised that for any one individual, change is unique to that person and occurs due to random social and environmental events. Some of these events are relatively common but others aren't. Examples include the effect that the following have on a person:

> relationships and breakdown of relationships

> having a serious illness or acquiring a disability

> being a victim of crime

> business failure (or success)

> significant promotion (or being made redundant)

> death of a close family member

There can be other unique events. Some individuals meet a charismatic person and so they embark on a totally new life direction (in lifestyle, work, spirituality etc).

In human development circles the randomness of life changing events has generated discussion about how much choice and control we actually have in our lives.

Hence, adult development models have identified three general influences on adulthood:

> There are some biological age related factors but these are mainly confined to changes that occur later in life

> There do appear to be generational factors as a result of societal pressures or opportunities

> The main influences in any one person's life are quite random but they can have a profound impact on a person's life direction.

In supervision discussion ask the student about how they
might draw on and apply theories of adult development in
their work:

> How do the theories of staged development support the
  student's understanding of where individuals are at and
  what the next stages are?

> How and why could development have been delayed for
  some vulnerable people the student may be working with?
  What impact has this had?

> How might anti-oppressive perspectives (and the theories
  covered in Section A) critique theoretical approaches to
  adult development?

> Critique what certain theories do not offer in terms of
  understanding the individual (e.g.: around generalising a
  diversity of experiences).

> What influence do society's and others' perceptions of
  "the norm" have upon how the individual is viewed and how
  they view themselves?

GRIEF AND LOSS

Models of grief and loss outline the experiences that people go through following a significant loss. The loss or bereavement may be anticipated or unexpected.

Some writers argue that people progress through recognisable stages. Other writers claim that people's responses are more fluid.

Accounts of grief and loss apply to bereavement (someone important to the person dying) and loss (a person experiencing a significant change that they didn't want such as losing a job, acquiring a disability etc.), although experiences of loss can be less intense.

Models of Grief

Kubler Ross (1969) argued that there were five stages of grief, these being:

➢ Denial. On first hearing of the person's death there may be disbelief. The person may hang on to the hope that the deceased will walk in as normal. Numbness and shock may also be felt.

➢ Anger. The strength of the pain results in anger; this anger can be directed at anyone, including self anger where the bereaved person blames themselves.

➢ Bargaining. Some people may try to negotiate with another person or with God to be given another chance, to be able to go back to how things were before.

➢ Depression. Once the person starts to absorb the full truth they may become deeply saddened. There can be intense feelings of loneliness and hopelessness. The person may be tearful over minor matters. They may have no energy for routine activities.

➢ Acceptance. There is no requirement that the deceased person is forgotten, but the bereaved person needs to recognise the truth of their situation and to gradually release their emotions. They will need to realise that they can carry on even if they still feel the loss of their loved one.

Bowlby (1980) has characterised the grief process as more dynamic. Bowlby listed four experiences but aspects of all of them could be

experienced by the bereaved person within the same week in any
order. The four processes are:

➤ Shock and numbness. Although this process is most likely to be
felt soon after the person is bereaved, it may be delayed due to the
person feeling they have to be strong (for the sake of others).

➤ Yearning and searching. The bereaved person may look for their
loved one. There could be experiences where the bereaved
person is sure they saw or heard the deceased person. This
process is sometimes referred to as 'pining'.

➤ Disorganisation and despair. This is the process that includes the
emotional turmoil that engulfs people who are bereaved.

➤ Reorganisation. The bereaved person starts to accept the loss
they have experienced and will need to establish their identity
afresh.

These are just two models and there are others. Even though these
approaches claim to be different, there are many similarities between
them.

Behaviours and Emotions

The range of behaviours and emotions that people experiencing grief
and loss display are extensive. All the literature makes it clear that
the individuality of the grieving process is to be respected. The pain
can be intense where the relationship was very close; a person could
feel relief if the relationship with the deceased was destructive.

Added to this is the cultural view of grief. In some cultures, grief is
very expressive and public; there is an expectation that the bereaved
will be in company for days to share their grief. In other cultures the
importance of privacy is emphasised.

The length of the grieving process is also very individual. However, it
is to be hoped that the bereaved person is able to function within four
to six weeks of the death of their loved one, even though their
emotional state may still be very raw.

In supervision discussion, ask the student to think more widely about aspects of grief and loss. Can any of the theories covered in this chapter, be applied to aspects of their work? For example, where a service user is denied a service (possibly due to the application of eligibility criteria) some aspects of the grief process can be identified.

The main point of attachment theory is that all children are born with an innate need to feel loved and wanted by their parents. If a child does not feel this, the child has a sense of emotional hurt that results in the child engaging in a range of behaviours that are intended to get the parent to love the child, but often the behaviours appear counter productive.

One of the fundamental needs of children to ensure optimal emotional and behavioural development, are secure attachments to the child's parents (or significant adult caregivers) from the beginning of their life.

Attachment theory was first promoted by Bowlby (1969, 1973, 1980). Since Bowlby first wrote about attachment many other writers have added to our knowledge. Examples include Ainsworth et al (1978); Rutter (1995), Belsky and Cassidy (1994). There are many more writers. The main impression to convey is that attachment theory is considered proved beyond reasonable doubt.

Every child has an innate need to feel loved and wanted by their parents. It is a parental responsibility to meet this need. Where attachments to parents are broken the child needs to have secure attachments established with alternative adult caregivers, ideally, before the child is aged 3, or as soon as possible after the attachment to the parent is ruptured.

Where a child has parents who do not make the child feel secure or where attachments have been ruptured there is a significant risk of the child having difficulty with a range of relationships and their problem solving and coping skills can be poorer. There is also a risk of the person, when they are adults (and parents), failing to provide secure attachments to their own children (and so the cycle continues).

The evidence around the effect of secure and insecure attachments is clear as secure attachments:

➤ Promote security

➤ Enhance a child's development of independence skills

➤ Foster a child's ability to establish social relationships

> Enable a child to explore and investigate the wider world
> Facilitate play as children develop and mature through play

Attachment theory makes clear that when a child senses that their attachments to their adult caregivers are not secure then they focus their emotions and behaviours on trying to re-establish their attachment (attachment behaviours are activated).

The child cannot engage in play and exploration when attachment behaviours are activated. The child's play shuts down (in terms of continuing to aid development).

The effect of this is clear. It is not unusual for a support worker or foster carer to notice that, say, a child aged 10 plays best with a 7 year old. Sometimes the foster carer or staff member may say the child appears immature for a 10 year old. This could be because the child has attachment anxieties.

Since the child is a child (obviously) then they do not have the language and emotional development of an adult. Therefore when attachment anxieties are triggered the child is not able to verbally express themselves. They express their attachment anxiety through their behaviours (attachment behaviours).

Attachment theory has established that there are three insecure types of attachment, each of which generates certain responses in the child (Howe et al, 2000).

1. Avoidant/Defended Attachment Anxiety

> Child rejected, may just be emotional rejection, but this rejection may include physical violence from the care giver
> Child downplays attachment
> Child minimises expressions of distress, the child knows that when their parent is shouting at them if the child is distressed this results in further parental rejection
> Child acts happy even when frightened
> Child shows aggression when they are dominant, e.g. at school with weaker children or with younger brother or sister

2. Ambivalent/Coercive Attachment Anxiety

➤ Unpredictable/insensitive care giving. Often characterised by neglect or disinterest in child. But there are times when child feels cared for and loved

➤ Child maximises expression of distress, especially when parent about to leave

➤ Child engages in attention seeking behaviour this can include the child ignoring the parent when back together, the child is communicating (but not saying verbally) "show me you love me"

➤ Child desires close relationships but is anxious over risk of withdrawal of affection. This can include child hanging around the parent for long periods of time

3. Disorganised/Controlling Attachment Anxiety

➤ A child finds this type of parenting the most difficult to adapt to

➤ Care givers are unpredictable and rejecting – this may just be emotional rejection but can include violence

➤ Care giver is frightening or frightened – a source of distress for the child. The care giver (parent) may have a drug or alcohol dependency or mental health problems. This affects the care giver's personality which causes the child distress

➤ If the child gets closer to care giver the child gets more distressed since the child becomes more aware of the impact of the parent's drug or alcohol dependency etc

➤ Child feels they are unloved and the child feels they are the cause of others anger

➤ Child flooded with emotions of fear and anger

➤ Child has fear of being in danger and feeling out of control, the child's behaviours can be inconsistent and destructive

➤ Only predictable aspect is the child, therefore they try to control themselves

➤ Child develops defences and inhibitions to maintain control

➤ Child can see themselves as strong, powerful but also bad. View of child as bad is impressed on child by parent who labels child as a bad child

➤ Child can stop fearing danger

> Child fears losing control – fears their feelings may overwhelm
> them. Child gives impression of being strong, assertive, even
> arrogant. This is a heavily defended façade. Behind the façade is
> emotional turmoil.

Attachment theory is often characterised as claiming that the first five
years of a child's life are crucial in terms of establishing secure
attachments. We would argue that attachment applies throughout a
child and young person's life. Indeed, there is increasing interest in
the way attachments affect adult behaviour (see Chapter 16).

There needs to be a clear awareness that attachment behaviours
change as the child becomes a young person, but the reason and
intention behind them remain the same.

A teenager who is experiencing ambivalent/ coercive attachment
anxiety is also likely to engage in attention seeking behaviour. Unlike
a seven year old, who may lie on the floor kicking and crying, a
teenager may engage in self-harm, sexual activity or consume alcohol
and then make sure that their parent is aware.

In supervision discussion, help the student to reflect on situations where attachment may be an issue, using questions such as:

> What behaviours is the child displaying which might be viewed as attachment behaviours?

> What actions could be taken to support the child to develop secure attachments?

> How might an understanding attachment theory help in you work with this situation?

Attachment theory is often something students will refer to in their portfolio or reflective accounts. Therefore, in addition, the practice assessor could work with the student to:

> Explore possible ways in which secure and insecure attachments may have affected the experience of one service user

> Explore HOW this theory may be applied to their own interactions with this individual and others supporting this person

> Consider WHY attachment theory offers insight, and how it links in with other theories (e.g.: learning theory, constructionism, labelling)

Attachment theory was developed from studying the relationships children had with their parents. In the last 15 years or so there has been increasing interest in the application of attachment theory to adults.

Attachment theory recognises that most adults have a basic need to feel loved and wanted by another adult. If an adult experiences rejection this can have an adverse effect on their ability to form and develop other relationships.

If an adult grew up feeling that they were not loved and wanted by one or both of their parents, then this could have a continuing impact on their ability to form stable relationships, both with other adults and with any children they then have.

It is difficult to predict exactly how an adult will respond. An adult who felt unloved as a child may, when they develop a romantic relationship, become completely dependent on that other adult. In many ways, this is fine so long as the relationship is long lasting. Another adult with a similar childhood experience may initially establish an intensive romantic relationship, but then break it abruptly.

The main 'escape' for an adult is that they become aware of how their childhood experiences are affecting their relationship with other adults. They need to become conscious of the sense of insecurity they have and why they behave in the way they do in their relationships with other adults (or their own children).

An adult needs to become conscious of their own insecurities. Then when they are in a situation in which their anxieties are triggered instead of responding unconsciously (e.g. promising never ending love or breaking the relationship entirely) they should be able to have some sense of choice as to how to respond. One response may be to discuss with their partner why they are experiencing the emotions they are presently feeling and what they would 'instinctively' do in response. The hope is that by being conscious and by being able to express themselves, whilst the adult may still feel insecure they can engage in behaviours which are less extreme and more controlled. In this way they are able to prevent situations occurring that appear to repeat previous situations in their life.

An adult may experience rejection due to some aspect that is part of them but which is devalued by society. Obvious examples are physical disability, learning disability or mental health problems.

The person with the disability or mental health problem may (and probably did) experience rejection as a child. They may not have been rejected by their parents (who may have been loving and caring) but the person may have experienced rejection either from individuals or through being treated differently, such as by being sent to a special school.

If the person had a positive childhood, there is still a risk that they will experience rejection and exclusion as an adult because they are seen as different (and not as good as others). They could then start to engage in behaviours that are an expression of their attachment anxieties. Owing to a fear of future rejection the person may show little or no interest in developing new relationships or going to new groups or organisations. The adult may say they are lonely and have no friends but the fear of rejection may leave them socially paralysed. Unfortunately, care staff can then label the person as lacking in self motivation or not taking responsibility for their own development etc.

If the adult is in a care service, the experience of the care service can compound and increase an adult's attachment anxiety. As with children, comments by staff (about ending shifts or taking leave), staff behaviours at work (clustering with other staff in an office, behind a closed door) and just the regular turnover of staff leaving, can all heighten a person's sense that they are still not loved and wanted for the person they are.

Sometimes when a new member of staff starts at a service, staff comment that a particular service user "tries it on" with the new staff member. Sometimes a service user may be aggressive to a new staff member. It could be argued that the service user is asking "Can I trust you?" Often the service user cannot sustain such a position (testing out the staff member) because of their own needs for support. Too often, however, the service user will find that they are let down by individual staff or the service.

An older person who has been cared for by a family member (partner, son or daughter) and has now had to enter a care home (against the service user's true wishes) could display attachment behaviours towards that family member when they are visited by the family member. Like so many attachment behaviours they appear counter productive. The older person in care may ignore their visitor, or they may be angry towards them. Rationally speaking, the service user should convey to the family member how important their relationship is to them and how hurt they feel now they are in a care service. However, such a rational perspective is the luxury of those who are not emotionally involved in a key relationship that always carried with it a sense of being loved, wanted and needed.

Attachment theory is often something students will refer to in their portfolio or reflective accounts. Therefore, in addition, the practice assessor could work with the student to:

> Explore possible ways in which secure and insecure attachments may have affected the experience of one service user

> Explore HOW this theory may be applied to their own interactions with this individual and others supporting this person

> Consider WHY attachment theory offers insight, and how it links in with other theories (e.g.: learning theory, constructionism, labelling)

LEARNING THEORY

17

Experiential Learning

Experiential learning is probably the main adult learning theory referred to in the social work arena. David Kolb (1984) is probably the most well known writer in experiential learning circles, although experiential learning can actually be traced back to 450BC when Confucius said:

> *"Tell me, and I will forget. Show me and I might remember. Involve me and I will understand."*

Experiential learning basically proposes that people learn based on an experience by going round a cycle of four stages. Kolb describes these as:

1.   Concrete Experience

2.   Reflective Observation

3.   Abstract Conceptualisation

4.   Active Experimentation

Along with many other theories, you can see that this is full of jargon but if you look beyond the language, the concept is quite straightforward.

This theory is often misunderstood by people – and taken to simply mean that people learn from experience. To some extent this is true, but the theory is that the experience is not sufficient in itself. Someone can have lots of experiences but learn nothing from them. The experience has to be followed by reflection and consolidation in order to learn effectively.

The cycle as presented by Kolb goes as follows:

1. Concrete Experience
    A person needs to have an experience to draw on – this could be doing something, reading something, having a conversation, ...pretty much anything really. The person won't necessarily

learn from the experience unless they move around the cycle, as follows:

2. Reflective Observation
   The person needs to reflect on the experience and make sense of it from a personal perspective. Then......

3. Abstract Conceptualisation
   Following on from the personally based reflection, the person needs to reflect more widely to make links with other experiences, prior knowledge, the wider context of the learning etc. This should help the person to move onto the next stage....

4. Active Experimentation
   The person develops a working hypothesis (if I do A, then B will happen) during this phase the hypothesis is tested out.

Other writers, such as Honey and Mumford (eg: 2000) have developed on from Kolb's cycle and present experiential learning in more accessible language, as demonstrated in the following diagram:

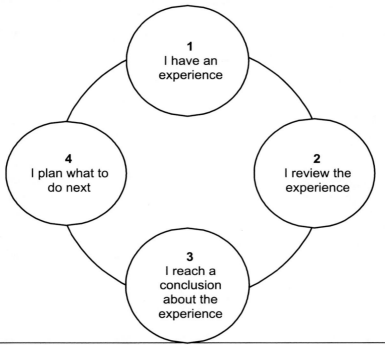

The most straightforward way of thinking about the learning cycle is to recognise that people only learn based on experience. However, the experience in itself will not be enough to ensure learning – just because you do something you won't necessarily learn from it. People have to continue round the cycle in order to learn from the experience. People may become "blocked" at any stage of the cycle which will impede their learning.

Reflective Practice

Reflective practice is closely linked to experiential learning – clearly reflection is an essential part of the learning cycle.

Schon (1987) states there are two types of reflection:

Reflection **IN** action
Reflection **ON** action

Reflection in Action

Reflection IN action is the process of reflection when you are actually doing something. Essentially, it is doing something and being aware of what you are doing at the same time. Reflection in action involves:

➢ Thinking ahead *(Right if that's happened, then I need to .....")*

➢ Being critical *("That didn't work very well....")*

➢ Storing up experiences for the future *("I could have dealt with that better, next time I will try....")*

➢ Analysing what is happening *("She's saying that to test me – I think I should....")*

Reflection in action is happening all the time – if your mind is on the job! This is important as not only is it good practice and respectful of service users, but it also constitutes reflection in action.

Whilst reflection in action is good practice and can help people to develop their practice, it does have drawbacks. The main problems are:

➢ You can only see things from your own perspective *("I think, I feel, I'm not sure....")*

copyright© Kirwin Maclean Associates Limited

➢ You will only have short term reflection. If your mind is on the
job, when the job changes so will your thoughts.

You can address these drawbacks by making sure that you also use
reflection ON action.

Reflection on Action

This is the reflecting you do after an event. Reflection ON action
refers to the process of thinking through and perhaps discussing the
incident with a colleague or a supervisor.

Reflection on action is free from urgency and any pressures of the
actual event. As such it allows for longer term reflection. You can
also ensure that by seeking feedback you use other people's
perspectives in your reflection.

The main drawback of reflection on action is that because of time
constraints we tend only to think in this way about more complex or
critical work issues. Therefore in terms of more routine events and
work practice, we tend only to "reflect in action". This can lead us to
not making much improvement in our routine work practice. It is
important therefore to plan reflection on action to ensure that it covers
every aspect of practice.

Planning to reflect rather than simply doing so when something has
gone wrong or been particularly difficult, is best practice. Planning to
reflect, along with reflection in action and some spontaneous (or
unplanned) reflection on action constitutes reflective practice.

Roth (1989) summarised the basic elements of a reflective
process as follows:

➢ Keeping an open mind about what, why and how we do things

➢ Awareness of what, why and how we do things

➢ Questioning what, why and how we do things

➢ Asking what, why and how other people do things

➢ Generating choices, options and possibilities

➢ Comparing and contrasting results

➢ Seeking to understand underlying mechanisms and rationales

> Viewing our activities and results from various perspectives

> Asking "What if....?"

> Seeking feedback and other people's ideas and viewpoints

Approaches to Learning

Honey and Mumford (eg: 2000) identified four different approaches to learning. These are not to be confused with the, more commonly known, four different learning styles – also developed by Honey and Mumford.

The Intuitive Approach

This involves learning through experience, but not through a conscious process. The person using the intuitive approach claims that learning is an inevitable consequence of having experiences. If questioned they are able to talk in detail about a variety of different experiences, describing what happened and what was achieved. The learning or developmental aspects are rarely, if ever, referred to. A person using the intuitive approach therefore finds it difficult to articulate what they have learnt or how they have learnt it. They are content that learning occurs through some 'natural' process of osmosis.

People who adopt the intuitive approach to learning are likely to say they have been to the "University of Life".

Since people using this approach put their trust in learning as a 'natural' effortless process, they find it difficult to accept that there are advantages to be gained by making the process more deliberate and conscious, either for themselves or for other people.

The Incidental Approach

This involves learning by chance from activities that jolt an individual into carrying out a 'post mortem'. Mishaps and frustrations often provide the spur.

When something hits people using the incidental approach, they are inclined to mull over what happened in an informal unstructured way. They may do this in odd moments such as travelling between appointments, driving home from work, or even sitting in the bath.

People using incidental learning tend to use the benefit of hindsight as a way of rationalising what happened.

People using the incidental approach often find it easier to conduct their post mortems by talking things over with someone else, preferably someone who was also present during the experience in question.

The Retrospective Approach

This involves learning from experience by looking back over what happened and reaching conclusions about it. In common with the incidental approach, the retrospective approach is especially provoked by mishaps and mistakes. In addition, however, people using this approach are more inclined to draw lessons from routine events and successes. They therefore extract learning from a diverse range of small and large, positive and negative experiences.

People using the retrospective approach conduct reviews, sometimes in their heads, sometimes in conversation and sometimes on paper. The sequence, slowed down, looks something like:

The Prospective Approach

This involves all the retrospective elements, but includes an additional dimension. Whereas retrospection concentrates on reviewing what happened after an experience, the prospective approach includes planning to learn before an experience. Future events are seen not merely as things to be done, but are viewed as learning opportunities.

The sequence in prospective learning is:

With the increasing professionalisation of social work, the prospective approach is being actively encouraged – it is often referred to as being proactive about your own learning. Increasingly, staff are asked to highlight their learning needs – either before accessing training or in their personal development reviews etc. This will be modelled in the practice assessor/student relationship, and students can transfer this to work with service users as part of anti-oppressive practice which enables individuals to reflect upon changes they make.

Learning Styles

Honey and Mumford (eg: 2000) developed the idea that people have different learning styles. They identified four different learning styles and designed a questionnaire which people can use to work out their style.

Activists

Activists are open minded and enthusiastic. They like new experiences and to get involved in the here and now. They are the kind of people who like to "get stuck in". They learn by doing. Activists can get bored once the activity stops and they prefer to look for the next experience rather than reflecting on what they have done.

Reflectors

Reflectors like to stand back and ponder things. They think about many different perspectives before acting. Reflectors like to "chew things over" before reaching any conclusions. Reflectors like to observe people, gather information and have plenty of time to think things over. They will learn best if given plenty of time to think about their responses.

Theorists

Theorists are basically logical thinkers. They like to analyse and question and learn in a step by step, logical way. Theorists will question any new learning and try to ensure it makes sense and fits in with their logical approach. Theorists can be perfectionists and can dislike a flippant approach.

Pragmatists

Pragmatists like to try out anything new to see if it works in practice. They like to take a problem solving approach to learning and are the kind of people who will try and apply something new that they have learnt straight away. If it doesn't work, they won't try it again!

Again, the learning styles questionnaire is something practice assessors often utilise at the start of a student placement, so that they can cater learning activities to the student's needs. However, it is worth considering how the student applies this in their work with service users around changing behaviours, so that a "one size fits all" approach is avoided.

Andragogy

Malcolm Knowles (1984) believes that most adult teaching has consisted of teaching adults as if they were children. He argues that adults are different from children as learners in three critical ways:

1. In terms of their self concept. Whereas a child first sees themselves as a completely dependent personality, the adult has developed a concept of themselves which values a certain degree of autonomy. Adults have a need to be perceived as self directing. The deepest need an adult has is to be treated as an adult, to be treated as a self directing person, to be treated with respect.

2. In terms of their experience. Whereas a child defines his or her self identity by reference to their family, school, community etc, adults usually define themselves in terms of their experiences. Self identity is derived from what we have done. Therefore adults are very jealous of the worth of our experience and wherever we find people devaluing our experience, not paying attention to it, not incorporating it in the education plan, we feel rejected as people.

3. In terms of their time perspective. Whereas in most aspects of life, a child's time perspective is one of immediacy and they find it hard to postpone the satisfaction of present desires, an adult is more accustomed to postponing immediate satisfactions. But in regard to learning, the time perspectives of children and adults is reversed. Children become used to learning things that will not have immediate application, but will be accumulated into a reservoir of knowledge and skills that will/may be useful in adult

life. But an adult's perspective in regard to learning is likely to be one of immediate application. According to Knowles the reason an adult enters into education is to be able to better deal with some life problem about which they feel inadequate now.

Knowles refers to the approach of teaching children as pedagogy and says that the teaching of adults should be based on a different approach which he calls andragogy. Andragogy should take account of the differences outlined above.

A critique of all of the theory on adult learning could take the position that children also do not exist as "empty vessels" waiting to be filled with knowledge (although that is how society often wants to see children). Child-centred educational practices focus on applying many of the concepts and principles of adult learning such as the need to know, motivation to learn, scaffolding onto prior experience and experiential learning. Many would argue that an overly traditional educational style which ignores these fails to differentiate between children as individual learners who have the ability to self direct and who learn better when these principles are applied. It should be remembered that the ideas in adult learning theory do not exclusively apply to adult experiences.

Dissonance

Cognitive dissonance was first written about in the 1950s by a psychologist named Leon Festinger (1957). It is used as a theory in a range of ways to understand people's behaviour, but it is most helpful as a theory of adult learning. The model is depicted below:

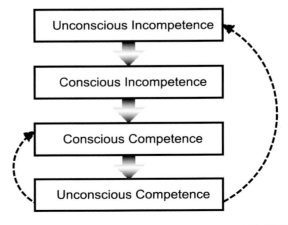

When we are called upon to learn something, say a new task, we all start in a position of being unconsciously incompetent (sometimes referred to as blissful ignorance). The idea is that we don't know what we don't know! As we begin to learn the new task, we become aware of what we don't know. We are now conscious of our incompetence! This is an uncomfortable time for most people – after all we are socialised to believe that there is "no such word as can't". Because of this discomfort, people can give up trying to learn the new task – avoiding the discomfort feels better than dealing with it. However, if people do stick with it and learn the new skill, they will move to the next stage of 'conscious competence.' The person can now do the task but they are very aware of it and very "conscious". If you have learnt to drive, you will probably recognise this phase – when you pulled away you probably said "mirror, signal, manoeuvre" if not out loud, certainly in your head.

Once we become familiar with a task, we move onto being 'unconsciously competent' – the task is so familiar we do it on 'automatic pilot'. The danger here is that people can slip into bad habits and not notice – they may go back to being 'unconsciously incompetent'. They are now doing the task badly or wrong but they are blissfully unaware. To return to the analogy of driving – most of us probably wouldn't pass our test if we sat it now. This means it is vital to keep alert about what we do and how we do it – which is where reflective practice comes in.

Social Learning Theory

One of the principle writers of social learning is Bandura (1977). Like so many theories, this is just describing a common life event.

Social learning describes the way that we engage in a behaviour because we have seen another person engage in the behaviour and that other person benefited from the behaviour (or they avoided something unpleasant happening to them). Social learning is more likely to be successful if the role model has status or standing with the learner and the new behaviour can be rewarded. Arguably, much of what we learn is through role modelling. This is most apparent in a parent/child relationship but there are lots of other examples.

Many teenagers and young adults learn social skills (and dating skills) from their peers through social learning. Many adults have learned other skills (such as computer skills) through watching others succeed at the task (in relation to computer skills, it is often their young child!).

Many self help groups and mutual support groups work on the basis of social learning and role modelling. Just one example is that of the Expert Patient Programme (EPP) (run in England). In the EPP, individuals with a long term health condition go on a training course where they learn how to manage their own condition as much as possible. One of the trainers is a person with the condition.

An understanding of adult learning theory will certainly help a student to understand and therefore maximise their own learning. However, it can also be useful to draw on an understanding of adult learning theory in work with service users. For example, the use of adult learning theory in group work is clear, helping people learn or re-learn essential skills – such as parenting or social skills can also be greatly assisted by adult learning theory.

Ask a student which adult learning theory they might have drawn on in their work with service users.

➢ How has their understanding of the theory assisted them in their work?

➢ What conclusions can they draw about the use of adult learning theory in social work?

ATTRIBUTION THEORY

18

Attribution theory is about how people interpret events and situations. It was first proposed by Heider in 1958 as a way of understanding and classifying the causes which people attribute to situations in life, and was developed further by Weiner (1974). Weiner linked the ideas more to the ways in which people learn and how they approach future tasks. This is based on attributions they have made about the successes and failures they have experienced before.

How people make attributions

The basic idea is that firstly an event happens or an individual does something and this is perceived by somebody else. Secondly, that individual then decides whether the act or event was deliberate or intentional or not. The third stage is that the person then attributes a cause or motivation for that event or action.

Attributions of cause can then be broken down as to whether they were as a result of:

➢ Something which was in the other person's control (internal attribution e.g.: intentional)

➢ Something which was a result of a situation out of their control (external attribution e.g.: luck)

Kelley (1967) argued that when we determine whether events or actions were intentional or not, we take into account:

➢ Consistency (does the person act this way every time they are in this situation)?

➢ Distinctiveness (does the person act this way in other situations)?

➢ Consensus (do other people act the same in the same situation)?

This is called the "covariation" model. Basically, when we decide if something has been done deliberately (either by ourselves or others), we ask these three questions. An example could be around deciding why a child misbehaves when they are with one parent. We would ask how often the child and parent feel there are difficulties (consistency), whether the child gets into trouble at school or when they are with the other parent (distinctiveness), and whether other siblings experience similar difficulties with this same relationship (consensus).

Attributing success

Weiner applied this to how people learn and he suggested four factors in how people decide on the causes for their success or otherwise in achievement. These factors are:

➢ Ability

➢ Effort

➢ Task difficulty

➢ Luck

Weiner's theory suggests that there are three "causal dimensions" which people use to classify the reasons they give for events or successes:

➢ Locus of control: is the success in a task because of a reason internal to the person, or because of something somebody else controls?

➢ Stability: does the cause change over time?

➢ Controllability: is the success because of a reason which is within the person's control such as effort, or is it because of a reason which cannot be controlled such as their ability?

We attribute our own successes or failures according to prior experiences. This theory therefore has a clear link with individuals' self esteem and identity.

For example, if someone does well, or not so well, in a test at school, they may attribute this to one of several reasons:

➢ I did well because I tried hard (internal, unstable, controllable)

➢ I did well because I am good at this subject (internal, stable, uncontrollable)

➢ I did well because I was lucky and the questions were easy (external, unstable, uncontrollable)

> I did not do well because I was unlucky (external, unstable, uncontrollable)

> I did not do well because the test was too hard (external, unstable, uncontrollable)

> I did not do well because I am no good at this subject (external, stable, uncontrollable)

How the person attributes their success or failure will influence how they approach similar tasks in the future. Again, this is based upon common sense, everyday experiences and the academic terms are not to confuse! We all do this as all human beings like to give reasons for everything, whether that be others' actions or our own achievements.

Lots of the literature in this area, suggests that people with high self esteem are more likely to be high achievers in education (and life). This is because they are more likely to attribute success to internal and controllable factors (such as their own effort), or internal, stable and uncontrollable factors (such as their own ability). Weiner suggests that these individuals are more likely to approach new situations with confidence, to try more difficult tasks out, and to be motivated to persist through difficulties (Heider 1958). The research suggests that people with low self esteem are more likely to attribute failure to factors outside of their own control.

There is a clear message within this for anyone working with vulnerable people as it is apparent that the messages we give people will reinforce positive or negative attributions. This links well with behavioural theory. For example, we are subject to messages all of the time in life about our own efforts, skills, abilities, aptitude and achievements (or lack of). If someone says to a child who is feeling really proud of something they have done that "You were lucky as that was easy for you", then that message, if reinforced by other similar types of statement will have an impact. Likewise, if someone hears repeatedly how hard they have tried and how proud they should be of their growing competence, then this is likely to have a positive effect. This applies with children, adults, colleagues, students and to ourselves.

There is some research as to the effectiveness of rewards as there is an indication within this theory that if somebody learns to behave in certain ways purely because they are expecting a certain reward, then they are more likely to attribute their success to factors outside of their own control. It could be argued then that rewards need to be used sparingly, and the rewards of praise may be more effective in supporting people to attribute successes to their own skills etc.

There is also much to suggest that as people we are more likely to attribute our own successes to factors within our control, and our failures to factors outside us. This is called a "Self serving bias" (Simmering 2008). However, working with vulnerable people the opposite may apply and the social work role may be to educate individuals, staff and families about this in order to build self esteem.

Application

Attribution theory is relevant in social work because people make decisions about each other based on how they perceive the actions of others. For example, a parent may attribute various causes to their child's difficult behaviours:

➢ They are naughty

➢ They are copying someone else (peers, another adult etc)

➢ They have been treated unfairly (e.g.: by a teacher)

➢ They are in a bad mood today (but do not normally behave in this way)

➢ They have been through a traumatic event

How social workers approach their interpretations of causal factors is clearly linked with attribution of behaviour. It is important therefore for students to understand the way this works.

The other way this theory is useful is around the fact that people's experience of success and failure in education, life experiences and relationships will have an impact upon how they approach situations.

Consider with the student a person they are working with
who they may have found challenging to engage or in terms of
the person's behaviour.

Using attribution theory, ask the following:

➢ What causes do they attribute to this person's
behaviour?

➢ What do other workers say about the person?

➢ How do reasons given and perceptions of this person link
to Kelley's theoretical framework?

➢ How could attribution theory help the student to link the
person's difficulties to self image and self esteem?

➢ What practical strategies does the theory offer for
building the person's sense of achievement?

D HOW THEORY INFORMS ASSESSMENT

"Although assessment has been recognised as a core skill in social work and should underpin all social work interventions, there is no singular theory or understanding as to what the purpose of assessment is and what the process should entail."
(Social Care Institute for Excellence 2003: 5)

With no single theory or approach to assessment, this section is potentially limitless. In order to clarify understanding, the section will look at assessment processes, concepts in assessment and models of assessment.

Assessment of needs is regularly referred to in the National Occupational Standards for Social Work (TOPSS 2003) see, for example, units 3, 7, 12, and 13. The ability to conduct assessments based within a sound framework of values and knowledge is essential for the student to be judged a competent practitioner.

Reading this section, you will learn more about:

➢ Assessment: Process Issues
➢ Models of Assessment
➢ Concepts of Need
➢ The Strengths Perspective and resilience
➢ Risk Assessment

FURTHER READING

This Guide provides an introduction to the main theories of social work. For further more detailed information on the areas covered in this section, see the following:

- Kemshall, H and Pritchard, J. (eds) (1996) *Good Practice in Risk Assessment and Risk Management.* (London) Jessica Kingsley.

- Milner, J and O'Byrne, P. (1998) *Assessment in Social Work.* (Basingstoke) MacMillan.

- Parker, J. and Bradley, G. (2003) *Social Work Practice: Assessment, Planning, Intervention and Review.* (Exeter) Learning Matters.

- Parsloe, P (ed) (1999) *Risk Assessment in Social Work and Social Care.* (London) Jessica Kingsley.

- Walker, S. and Beckett, C. (2003) *Social Work Assessment and Intervention.* (Lyme Regis) Russell House Publishing.

In terms of process, there are two main areas to consider:

➢ the assessment process
➢ assessment as part of a process

<u>The Assessment Process</u>

In considering the assessment process, Milner and O'Bryne present a five stage model of assessment (1998):

Stage 1: Preparation – which might include deciding who to see, what the purpose of the assessment is, what information will be needed etc.

Stage 2: Data collection – the worker gathers the necessary information.

Stage 3: Weighing up the data – the worker weighs up the information to reach an answer to the key question "is there a problem and is it serious?"

Stage 4: Analysing the data – the information is interpreted to gain a fuller understanding so that ideas for intervention can be developed.

Stage 5: Utilising the data – this stage is used to finalise judgements. The data will be used to evidence judgements and recommendations for intervention.

Assessment is presented as part of a wider overall process of social work in many texts. The process is generally seen in a similar way, as the start of the process, referred to by Taylor and Devine (1993) as the "basic helping cycle", illustrated in the following:

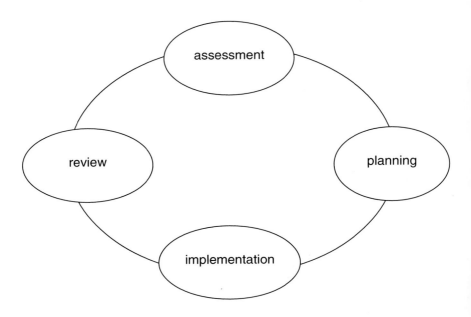

Others build on this idea by developing specific processes:

➤ The ASPIRE model (Sutton 1999)

        AS -   Assessment
        P   -   Planning
        I   -   Intervention
        RE -   Review and Evaluation

➤ The ASIRT model (Thompson 2005)

        AS -   Assessment – which acts as the basis of an action
                plan which informs the:
        I   -   Intervention – assessment sets the objectives for
                the intervention.
        R   -   Review – assessment becomes the baseline from
                which the review/evaluation operates.
        T   -   Termination – assessment objectives are
                considered in terminating intervention.

More recently however, some writers have started to dispute this, claiming that assessment can be an end in itself and doesn't necessarily lead to any intervention – therefore the "cycle" is not always followed. If the assessment is good enough, then some people will be able to act on it for themselves and will not require further services. The assessment then IS the service which is provided.

"While assessment is sometimes viewed as preceding intervention, increasingly assessment is being seen as a service in its own right rather than as a prelude to service delivery."

(SCIE 2003:2)

Theory and Assessment: The Links

Theory can be used in assessment in a variety of ways. To illustrate this, it is helpful to return to the 5 stage model of assessment proposed by Milner and O'Byrne (1998).

Theory can be utilised at any of the stages and the practitioner's choice of theory could have a significant impact on the assessment and any subsequent plans, as follows:

Preparation. The practitioner's choice of theory is likely to impact on factors such as who they want to see, what type of information they deem necessary etc. So that for example, if a worker favours systems theory, they will probably plan to gather information not only from the service user but also from family members, other professionals etc.

Data Collection. The worker's choice of theory can affect the questions they ask and the way they gather the information. For example, some practitioners always use the miracle question (see Chapter 26) as part of their assessment process. Clearly where a worker adopts a biographical or narrative approach to their assessment this will affect the evidence that the worker gathers.

Weighing up and analysing the data. Here a practitioner will draw on a range of different theories – often more than one in any given assessment in order to make sense of all of the information they have gathered. If theory is not applied in some way at this point then the worker simply has a jumble of information which may or may not link together and which may or may not make sense.

Utilising the data. The way the information gathered in an assessment is utilised will depend on the theory or theories that the worker has applied in interpreting the data.

As covered in Section A, a theory is viewed as helping to:

> ➤ Describe (e.g.: it answers the question "What is happening?")
> ➤ Explain (e.g.: it answers the question "Why is it happening?")
> ➤ Predict (e.g.: it answers the question "What is likely to happen next?")
> ➤ Control and/or bring about change (e.g.: "How can I change what may happen next?")

In many ways these four points link to the stages of assessment as presented by Milner and O'Byrne which helps to clarify the way that theory and assessment are inextricably linked.

This links to the theory circles which we explored in Section A. Any assessment which a student (or worker) formulates and any resulting plans will be based upon the individual's interpretation of what that person needs, what services can be provided and what the person can do for themselves. This will be influenced by the student's prior experiences, their values, the ways in which opinions about the person's needs are expressed, the student's awareness of resources, and the student's basis of knowledge in theory.

This process will clearly be influenced by the agency context within which the student's placement is set. It would be no use for example for the student to offer services which the placement setting does not support within its framework. The practice assessor and/or the placement supervisor will also influence the student's thinking around how needs are assessed and what resulting services the person can receive.

The student needs to be able to weigh up the person's needs against the following issues in order to reach a competent assessment:

> ➤ How the service user(s) and carer(s) state their own view of what is needed
> ➤ The views of other professionals
> ➤ The service context and view of colleagues, supervisors etc

➢ Theoretical knowledge and evidence bases of what works

To help the student make further links between assessment,
the social work process and theory present the student with
situations similar to the following and use supervision
discussion to cover the suggested questions.

Children's Services

Consider the example of a child who is getting into trouble in
the community, at risk of school exclusion, at risk of family
breakdown and who has been experiencing problems at home
with parental conflict. This is an example which may often
present in family support services, voluntary sector settings,
YOTs etc, consider how an assessment and plan might develop.

What would be the pros and cons of the following approaches
being taken?

➢ A medical model where the child's behaviour is "treated"

➢ A model focusing on the child's disempowerment as a
member of society

➢ A model focusing on attachment between the child and
their parents

➢ A parenting approach based on management of behaviour
at home, role modelling and parental relationships

➢ A model based on building the child's self esteem, social
and support networks

How might approaches differ between different work
settings?

Are there any ways in which the student's assessment could
combine the best of several approaches?

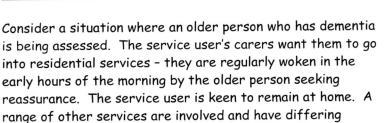

Adult Services

Consider a situation where an older person who has dementia is being assessed. The service user's carers want them to go into residential services – they are regularly woken in the early hours of the morning by the older person seeking reassurance. The service user is keen to remain at home. A range of other services are involved and have differing perspectives on what should be the outcome for the service user.

What would be the pros and cons of the following approaches being taken:

➤ A medical model where the older person is 'treated'.

➤ A model focussing on empowering the older person

➤ A model focussing on attachment between the older person and their family

➤ A systems approach looking at the older person's support network

➤ A behaviourist approach looking at managing the older person's contacts with their family members

How might approaches differ between different work settings?

Are there any ways in which the student's assessment could combine the best of several approaches?

Feel free to amend the situations offered for discussion to fit the student's experiences.

MODELS OF ASSESSMENT

In research published in 1993 Smale and Tuson (et al) identified three different models of assessment which are still seen as the three main models of assessment in social care services:

➤ The Questioning Model

Here, the worker holds the expertise and follows a format of questions, listening to and processing the answers. The use of this model means that the assessment process largely reflects the worker's agenda.

➤ The Procedural Model

Using this model, the worker gathers information to make a judgement about whether the service user fits the criteria for service provision. It is likely that a range of checklists will be used. The use of this model means that the assessment process largely reflects the agency agenda.

➤ The Exchange Model

In this model, workers view people as experts on their own problems. The emphasis of this model is on exchanging information. The worker follows what people are saying rather than trying to interpret what they think is meant. The worker should help the service user to identify internal resources and potential. In this way the practitioner can consider how best to help service users mobilise their own resources in order to reach goals which are defined by the service user. The use of this model means that the assessment should reflect the service user's agenda.

Smale et al make it clear that the exchange model is their preferred model. Working to this model however requires a great deal of skill. It means more than merely sharing assessments with service users. The model asserts that people in need and their family and friends will always know more about their problems and how they affect them, than workers. However, the model recognises that workers will have expertise in the process of problem solving. The aim of the worker should be to involve people in arriving at a compromise for ensuring needs are met. Rather than "making" an assessment the worker should manage the process.

Whilst making clear that they favour the exchange model, Smale et al acknowledge that workers can often feel pushed into the procedural model of assessment when they feel overwhelmed by agency pressures, eligibility criteria and the scarcity of resources. However, they point out that the exchange model can still be useful in these situations as long term and more stable solutions are likely to be reached, and because inner resources can be maximised so that resource provision can be limited to specific areas (if needed at all).

Smale et al accept that the questioning model is the most likely to be used when risk is the main emphasis of the assessment. Since specific answers to questions will be needed and to some extent the worker's agenda will need to be addressed.

It is our view that often students begin the development of their assessment skills by using a questioning or procedural model. Often they are so overwhelmed by the paperwork, that they focus on the accurate completion of this – leading them away from an exchange model. As the student's confidence grows, they may be able to work more towards an exchange model of assessment. Discussion of these models of assessment in supervision can certainly assist them in developing their assessment skills.

It is useful to reflect on shadowing experiences the student may have had with other agencies and colleagues. This offers a safe environment for the student to reflect consciously on what they have seen, what they felt worked well, and how they might apply this to their own practice.

How have the student's shadowing experiences allowed them to witness the models described in this chapter?

What does the student think would work for them and what approaches would they adapt in their own practice?

How much of the practice they have shadowed is influenced by the agency's context and procedures, and where does the student feel best practices can be followed within necessary limitations?

"Needs Led" Assessment

In recent years an emphasis has been put on needs led assessment. Many would argue that as the people carrying out assessment are often employed by agencies with limited resources that assessment can never be truly needs led. There are further arguments that the concept of need in itself is not clear, so it is worth developing an overview of theories of need.

There are a number of theories of need. Perhaps the most well known of which is Maslow's hierarchy of needs.

Maslow's Hierarchy of Needs

Maslow (1970) argues that all humans have a hierarchy of needs. We first need to satisfy basic biological needs (eg food, warmth etc) and then we are successively drawn to meet higher needs.

Originally Maslow created a pyramid of needs with five levels. He later extended this to seven levels.

The Strength of the Needs

Maslow argued that each level of need was a very powerful motivating force for each person.

At first, we are preoccupied with meeting our physiological (or biological) needs. If our need for food, water, warmth etc is not being met, then all the other 'higher' needs are unimportant. We must satisfy our biological needs. Once we are in a situation where our biological needs are largely or fully met, we start to experience a craving for safety and security. The more fully our biological needs are met, the stronger is our desire to establish safety and security. The safety and security needs are not just about being free of the fear of being physically attacked. It also refers to our need for stability, order and routine. This includes social and economic stability.

Once the safety and security needs are largely or fully met, then our
need for belonging and love becomes as intense as the two
preceding needs once were. We crave the opportunity to love and to
be loved, to belong to someone else, to be part of a wider group or
community.

When we satisfy or largely meet our need to love and be loved, the
importance of our need for self esteem starts to rise in importance.
This need includes being able to achieve tasks, being competent,
independent and having personal strength. Additionally, we need
respect from others in the form of prestige, status – even fame.
Maslow noted that basing self esteem solely on the opinion of others
was inviting insecurity. We need a sense that self esteem is based
on deserved respect from others rather than celebrity or unwarranted
adulation.

The need for self actualisation increases as our need for esteem is
satisfied. Maslow assumes that all people will experience this need.
How this need is satisfied will be an expression of our individuality.
For one person, it will be through being an ideal mother; for another
person, achieving a physical, athletic goal; for yet a different person,
developing a new invention etc.

In his later writings, Maslow then added on two higher stages. In
some respects they are extensions of the self actualisation stage
rather than entirely new stages.

In the first of the two new stages (the sixth stage of the whole
pyramid) Maslow argued that we have a need to know, to be curious
to seek to understand our world. People who enter into boring,
unstimulating lifestyles are at risk of developing mental health
problems.

The second of the two new stages (the seventh stage of the whole
pyramid) is the aesthetic need. Maslow recognised that this need
may only be felt by some people. However, for these people the
need to experience beauty, symmetry and idealised harmony was so
strong that Maslow felt it should be considered a need.

Maslow made clear that people did not need to work through the
stages in a methodical, rigid manner. A person could be seeking to
meet their needs from two or three stages at the same time. But a

person would only be able to increasingly devote their personal
resources to a higher stage once a lower stage was largely satisfied.

The Pyramid of Needs

Aesthetic Needs Some
people have a need to
see or experience
beauty, symmetry in art,
environment, music etc

To Know and Understand We have a
need to know, to understand and to
explain.

Self Actualisation Need Need for self fulfillment to
reach potential.

Esteem Needs To have self respect, self esteem and to have
esteem from others.

Belongingness and Love needs To give and receive love, to belong in a
family, group, clan or nation.

Safety and Security Needs Physical safety but also law and order, social stability,
continuity, job security etc.

Physiological (or Biological) Needs such as the need for food, warmth, drink, sleep

Perspectives on Maslow's Hierarchy of Needs

Maslow's Hierarchy of Needs has been a very significant standard in seeking to explain human motivation and the human condition. It is incredibly popular.

Within psychology, it has been difficult to generate research that can adequately test the theory. Some psychologists like the theory so much they have developed it further, either by increasing or reducing the number of stages. Other psychologists have pointed out its weakness and the way there are individuals who do not follow the staged progression.

Maslow's Hierarchy of Needs and Services

There are too many services that only support service users as far as level two. Some services don't even get as high as level two (safety and security). Very few service users are actively supported to have their needs around love and belonging met. Additionally, the use of labels in services cuts across upholding a person's self esteem and their sense that others respect them as competent people.

Human Needs Theories

Whilst Maslow's hierarchy is perhaps the most well known theory of need, there are others. A number of writers have developed Maslow's ideas. One of the most well known is John Burton who has developed Maslow's hierarchy to apply it to theories about human conflict. Burton sees human needs not as a hierarchy but more as an emergent collection of human development essentials. These needs do not have a hierarchical order. Rather, they are sought simultaneously in an intense and relentless manner (Burton 1990).

Burton and other human needs theorists categorise needs in areas such as:

➤ Safety/security

➤ Belongingness/love

➤ Self esteem/personal fulfilment

➤ Identity

➤ Cultural security

> Freedom

> Justice

> Participation

Bradshaw's Taxonomy of Need

First developed by Jonathan Bradshaw in relation to the needs of older people, this was entitled a taxonomy of social need (see 1972). However, it is now probably more widely used in terms of health care than social care.

Bradshaw refers to real need. He believes this to be a combination of four types of need:

> Normative need. This refers to needs which the expert/professional defines – these needs tend to be based on the professional's view of societal 'norms'.

> Perceived/felt needs. This refers to needs felt by the individual – in a way a self assessment. This type of need is sometimes referred to as a "want" rather than a need.

> Expressed need (demand). This refers to the needs expressed by people – this can be seen as felt need converted into expressed need when the person seeks assistance.

> Comparative need. This refers to the comparison that people make in defining needs – do we need what others have? etc. This is often referred to in understanding poverty – the concept of comparative poverty recognises that people may perceive themselves to be poor in comparison with others but this would not necessarily be viewed as "real" poverty.

Bradshaw claims that each of these areas of need overlaps and that it is perhaps somewhere in the overlap that "real need" can be found. (Glendinning et al 2005)

Acquired Needs Theory

Proposed by McClelland (e.g.: 1961) this theory is also known as learned need theory or the three need theory. The idea is that we all have needs which fall into three general categories:

> Achievement (coded as N-Ach)

➢ Affiliation (coded as N-Aff)

➢ Power (coded as N-Pow)

McClelland proposed that a person's specific needs are acquired over time and are shaped by life experiences. He goes on to say that most people feel that one of these needs is more important than the others. As such, he says which one of these is most important to us most affects our behaviour. Thus, he states that there are three types of people:

➢ Achievers

➢ Affiliation seekers

➢ Power seekers

This theory of need has been particularly influential in terms of understanding people at work and within organisations.

Outcomes Focussed Assessment

The concept of needs led assessment is now being complimented by outcomes focussed assessment. This has been developed by research carried out at the University of York. This approach is based on the social model of disability and empowerment (Harris et al 2005).

The approach identifies outcomes in three dimensions.

➢ outcomes involving change – for example improving self confidence, self-care skills or changes to accessibility of environments

➢ outcomes that maintain quality of life (or slow down deterioration in quality of life.) Sometimes referred to as maintenance outcomes.

➢ outcomes that are associated with the process of receiving services – such as feeling valued, being respected, feeling listened to etc.

Harris et al (2005) have developed an outcomes framework which categorises outcomes into four areas – in many ways these four areas could be seen as needs. The three dimensions of outcomes could be applied to any of the four areas in the framework.

Autonomy Outcomes	Personal Comfort Outcomes
➢ Access to all areas of the home ➢ Access to locality and wider environment ➢ Communicative access ➢ Financial security	➢ Personal hygiene ➢ Safety/Security ➢ Desired level of cleanliness of home ➢ Emotional well-being ➢ Physical health
Economic Participation Outcomes ➢ Access to paid employment as desired ➢ Access to training ➢ Access to further/higher education/employment ➢ Access to appropriate training for new skills (e.g.: lip reading)	**Social Participation Outcomes** ➢ Access to mainstream leisure activities ➢ Access to support in parenting role ➢ Access to support for personal secure relationships ➢ Access to advocacy/peer support ➢ Citizenship

The outcomes focussed approach is seen as a user centred approach which involves the practitioner acting more as facilitator than assessor.

Research carried out by the Social Policy Research Unit (Harris et al 2005) identified that many professionals find an outcome focussed approach to be an improvement on needs based assessment.

➤ A range of discussion points can be drawn out from
Maslow's hierarchy:

Maslow's theory could be a very helpful measure for
students in assessing individual's needs e.g.: with
children experiencing difficulties or in seeking to
develop person centred care for vulnerable adults. The
pyramid provides students with clearly identifiable
stages that they could support service users to progress
through.

The pyramid could also be used to evaluate (even if only
in broad measure) the quality of service provision.

How can a student's planning support each service user
to work through the levels and achieve their own goals
as fully as possible?

➤ Ask the student to consider whether agency assessment
processes and practice focus more on needs led or
outcomes focussed assessment. They should evidence
their response by discussing the differing approaches.
Why might the agency prefer this process?

➤ Which approach does the student favour and why?

➤ How might other theories of need influence service
provision?

THE STRENGTHS PERSPECTIVE
AND RESILIENCE

22

The strengths perspective is not a theory in itself. It has been developing for many years (arguably at least 40 years) with different writers contributing to its formation from their own fields.

The strengths perspective is partly a reaction against two features of traditional social work and the provision of health and social care.

1. An increasing medical classification and diagnosis of individuals leading to labelling of large sections of society. This labelling is negative and has a deterministic theme (e.g.: you had a traumatic childhood <u>therefore</u> you will be a terrible parent and your children will end up in care).

2. Assessments of needs have always been weighted towards listing people's deficits, vulnerabilities and negative past experiences. In the current environment where demand for services is increasing but the resources available have barely increased, then there is an increased focus and heightening of service users' lack of capability and risks.

In both of these suggestions, there is a structural or bureaucratic bias against recognising people's strengths, abilities and resilience. Professionals may be led to make use of a language that is pathologising and alienating in order to ensure that service users have access to services.

Saleebey (1996) generated the following comparison of professional pathologising against the strengths perspective.

Pathology	Strengths
Person is defined as a 'case'; symptoms add up to a diagnosis.	Person is defined as unique; traits, talents, resources add up to strengths.
Therapy is problem focussed.	Therapy is possibility focussed.
Service user accounts are filtered by a professional to aid the generation of a diagnosis.	Personal accounts are the essential route to knowing and appreciating the person.
Professional is sceptical of personal stories and explanations.	Professional knows the person from the inside out.
Childhood trauma is the precursor or predictor of adult dysfunction.	Childhood trauma is not predictive; it may weaken or strengthen the individual.
Professional devises treatment or care plan.	Focus is aspirations of individual, family or community.
Professional is the expert on service user's life.	Individual, family or community are the experts.
Possibilities for choice, control, commitment and personal development are limited by label/diagnosis or condition.	Possibilities for choice, control, commitment and personal development are open.
Professionals knowledge, skills and connections are principle resources for service user.	The strength, capacities and adaptive skills of the individual, family or community are the principle resources.
Support is centred on reducing the effects of symptoms and the negative effects of emotions or relationships	Support is focussed on getting on with one's life, affirming and developing values and commitments and making or finding membership in a community.

The strengths perspectives argue that personal qualities and strengths can come out of and be formed by difficult life experiences. Resilience, independence, loyalty to one or more people can arise due to a painful or traumatic personal experience. People can develop great insight into their own situation.

An important source of strength can be cultural, community or personal stories or narratives. Cultural or community accounts of origins, development, migration and survival can provide inspiration and meaning (Saleebey, 1996).

Most professionals will probably say that they already apply the strengths perspective to their work. The counter to this is that many professionals only pay lip service to the strengths perspective. This is because the strengths perspective calls on the professional to move away from the objective, concrete and tangible. The strengths perspective calls on the professional to connect with the individuals and families they work with in a manner that recognises hope, aspirations, spirituality, identity and belonging. The connection needs to be rooted in a true sense of equality.

The strengths perspective recognises that individuals and families have already been subjected to a range of demanding life events. Additionally, if people have had contact with health and social work services for some time they could have internalised the ideas of deficiency and needs. It is in addressing this that the professional's skills are called upon to work creatively with the service user and this can be very demanding. Individuals who have lived with grinding poverty or are on guard due to intimidatory and unpredictable racism are not going to automatically refer to the way they have benefited from their life experiences. The social worker is required to enable the service user to recognise the talents, resources, adaptive skills and support network the service user or family has.

Resilience Perspective

The resilience perspective is closely related to the strengths perspective. Often resilience is seen as one aspect of the strengths perspective.

Resilience refers to supporting people develop their own reservoir of skills, abilities and knowledge. This personal reservoir includes the person's social support network. Ideally the individual's sense of the resources they have should be developed in depth (eg: strengthening existing family relationships or friendships) and across a broad range (the person is supported to try new experiences both so that they acquire new skills but also such that they meet new people).

The resilience perspective recognises that individuals can have difficulties in one area of their life. One of the ways a person overcomes a difficulty is by drawing on other aspects of their life either directly to problem solve, or indirectly so that the person has a sense that in other areas of their life they are doing well.

Development of the Strengths Perspective

Each branch of social care and social work has developed its own literature on recognising people's strengths. For example:

In mental health services, the recovery model is closely related to aspects of the strengths perspective:

➢ The focus on wellness rather than illness

➢ The recognition of a person's individuality

➢ The de facto acknowledgement of the effects of the person's mental health problems but a recognition of the fact that this doesn't stop the person getting on with life

➢ Maintaining a sense of hope

In learning disability services, the strength's perspective (although not called that at the time) can be seen as far back as the 1960s.

➢ Jean Vanier has consistently talked about how much he learnt from people with learning disabilities he lived with, the strengths of people, the way his life has been enriched by living with people with learning disabilities etc (eg: Vanier 1988)

➢ Wolfensberger has been ambivalent towards professionals due to their failure to recognise the strengths of people with learning disabilities (eg: Wolfensberger 1988)

➢ Numerous other writers have championed the importance of engaging with people with learning disabilities as true equals and to recognise the way society benefits (eg: Brandon 1997, Neufeldt 1990, Williams 2006 etc).

In children's services the strengths and resilience of black families has been focussed on by various researchers who have been concerned by the way services have applied institutional racism in their work with black families:

➢ Owusu-Bempah and Howitt (1999) have discussed how black children can develop a positive sense of self in spite of racism and the importance of family relationships generally.

> Hylton (1997) discusses survival strategies used by black families who experience racism including the importance of the whole (wider) family and spirituality.

> Dutt and Phillips (2000) convey the importance of recognising the strengths of black families.

These are just examples, but it is sufficient to say that the strengths perspective has advocates in all areas of social care and social work.

Limitations and Critique of the Strengths Perspective

There is no acknowledgment of reluctant or resistant service users. Some service users don't want contact with services. Also some service users are not honest with social workers or social care staff. Due to this, many workers adopt a sceptical approach to what service users say. The worker may take the service user's account seriously but they then test it, either through further questions or by seeking independent confirmation from someone else. Such professional scepticism cuts across the strengths perspectives sense of values. In theory the worker needs to generate an environment where the service user or family member feels they can be honest. However, if the service user or family member declares they have harmed a child or vulnerable adult, then the worker will have to initiate various actions.

The extent of illness or life trauma is minimalised. There is no intention to gloss over difficulties in a person's life. Cousins (1989) said that one should not deny the verdict (medical diagnosis, assessment etc) but should defy the sentence. A radical social perspective would question the societal move towards increased labelling. Rather than being defined by a label, it can be more productive to discuss with the person in what ways their hopes and aspirations are being restricted or limited. What are the practical impacts? What are the impacts on motivation, outlook and personal ambitions? Then move from there.

The strengths perspective presents workers and students
with both a challenge and an opportunity. To apply the
strengths perspective fully they must move away from
bureaucratic, deficit led assessments. The student needs to
engage with the service user or family in the language of
hope, aspirations and redemption (good things come out of
painful experiences). As a suggestion, practice re-framing
statements about problems into being ones about learning
from difficulties.

Ironically, the opportunity is that in a time of increasingly
restricted services, the student who engages with an
individual or family and supports them identify the strengths
and abilities they have in themselves and their support
network will leave the service user or family with something
to build on.

Reflect in supervision discussions how the student applies
this learning to their work.

RISK ASSESSMENT

23

Risk assessment is a key aspect of social work practice. For example see the National Occupational Standards for Social Work (TOPSS 2003) units 4 and 12, and the GSCC Codes of Conduct 2002 Sections 3 and 4. To understand the concept of risk assessment and the theoretical underpinning to this, it helps to understand that risk assessment is generally carried out in terms of two areas:

➤ The risks a person poses to others (dangerousness)

➤ The risks a person is subject to (vulnerability)

Whatever the focus of the assessment, the purpose is generally for the assessment to inform plans about intervention – generally referred to as risk management strategies.

The Risks a Person Poses to Others

In these situations risk assessment views risk as wholly negative and the focus is on accurately assessing the risks posed such that they can be avoided. Examples of this form of assessment are drawn from assessment of offending behaviour by workers in the criminal justice system or assessments by workers in mental health teams where a person is felt to pose a risk to others.

The Risks a Person is Subject to

Risk assessment in these situations doesn't necessarily focus on risk as wholly negative. There is a recognition that risk taking can be positive – eg: in increasing skills, developing confidence etc. Here the focus is on identifying risks then deciding which risks are acceptable and which are not acceptable.

The assessment should lead to strategies for risk management which focus on balancing the benefits of risk taking with any potential harm.

Interestingly, it can be argued that risk assessment in terms of child protection and, to an increasing extent, adult protection combine aspects of dangerousness and vulnerability assessments. So that for

example a risk assessment may explore the "vulnerability" of the child
and the "dangerousness" of the care giver.

Two basic techniques are used in risk assessments:

➤ Actuarial Assessment
➤ Clinical Assessment

Actuarial Assessment

This is developed from insurance industry methods for risk calculation
and is basically about a statistical calculation of risk. The focus is on
probabilities which are expressed in numerical terms – usually
percentages or scores as with the ASSET format which is used by
Youth Offending Services.

Actuarial assessment is seen as more accurate than clinical
assessment but there are always problems with statistical measures.
The approach is reliant on research findings about groups and it can
be difficult to transfer learning from generalised information to
individual situations. Therefore the more infrequent the risk, the less
accurate the actuarial prediction will be.

Actuarial assessment is limited in terms of risk management solutions
in that this type of assessment provides a prediction about likelihood
rather than offering any understanding about the risks, possible
effects etc.

Clinical Assessment

Clinical assessment is a much more individual assessment method.
It is undertaken by workers on a case by case basis. Clinical
assessment is based on a professional judgement of risk and as such
can be value based and subjective. Clinical risk assessment has a
poor record of accuracy.

It is largely accepted that there are two forms of error with clinical
assessment – false negatives and false positives (see the following
page).

Despite the unreliability of clinical assessment, it does have some
strengths, in that this individualised form of assessment can offer
more than simple probability predictions. This type of assessment

can provide an analysis which offers an understanding of the nature
of risk and ideas for risk management strategies.

Holistic Risk Assessment

Recognising that neither of these two approaches are wholly
effective, writers now promote an approach which combines the
positives of each method (e.g.: Limandri and Sheridan, 1995,
Kemshall, 2002). This holistic approach combines probability
predictions and ideas about the nature of the risk. These combined
methods are often referred to as "second generation" assessment
tools (Monahan and Steadman 1994). Kemshall sees the holistic
approach to risk assessment as essential to individual case work.
She sees this approach as highlighting areas for significant
intervention and change as part of the care management process
(Kemshall 2002).

Conclusions and Decisions in Risk Assessment

No risk assessment process can be totally accurate. As previously
stated both actuarial approaches and clinical approaches are not "fail
safe".

It is generally accepted that there are two types of inaccuracies –
false positives and false negatives. The following table taken from
Walker and Beckett (2005: 86) clarifies this.

True and false positives and negatives

True positives	Situations identified as high risk where the harmful event actually occurs in the absence of protective intervention.
False positives	Situations identified as high risk where the harmful event actually would not occur even in the absence of protective intervention.
True negatives	Situations identified as low risk where no harmful event occurs.
False negatives	Situations identified as low risk, but where the harmful event does nevertheless occur.

This table is helpful in that it illustrates how, when carrying out a risk
assessment and planning intervention, a worker can "go wrong" in
two ways. For example, let's take a situation where a child is

removed from her parents' care because a risk assessment has concluded that she is at risk of significant harm. Using the concept of true and false negatives and positives there are 2 potential outcomes:

True Positive — If the child would have remained in her parents care, she would have been harmed ie: the assessment and intervention was "right".

False Positive — If the child had remained at home, she would not have come to any harm ie: the assessment and intervention was "wrong". In actual fact, since the removal of the child will in itself cause distress and 'harm' to the child further harm has been caused.

In another situation a child is left in the care of his parents because a risk assessment has concluded that there is a low risk of harm. Again there are 2 potential outcomes:

True negative — The child remains at home and comes to no harm ie: the risk assessment was "right".

False negative — The child remains at home and is harmed ie: the assessment was "wrong".

Understanding the concept of true and false positives and negatives helps to illustrate the double bind that social work and social care staff often find themselves in. "Damned if you do, damned if you don't." This has led to various discussions about decision making, and as a result of these Carson (1996) introduced the concept of defensible decision making.

Defensible Decision Making

In recognition of the fact that risk assessment is a highly fallible process, with no guarantee of certainty, Carson argues that the key skill is to arrive at decisions in a manner that a reasonable body of co-professionals would also have followed. This makes the decision defensible if brought to account.

Aspects that make up a defensible decision include:

➢ all reasonable steps are taken

> reliable assessment methods have been used
> information is collected and thoroughly evaluated
> decisions are recorded
> staff work within agency policies and procedures
> staff communicate with others and seek information they do not have

The Hindsight Fallacy

Introduced by Macdonald and Macdonald (1999) this concept is in common language ("in hindsight..." "with the benefit of hindsight..." etc). When a negative result occurs – for example a risk assessment has concluded a low risk and then a child is harmed, the assumption is that a serious mistake has been made. However, this is not always the case. The risk assessment may have led to a highly "defensible decision".

"....a bad outcome in and of itself does not constitute evidence that the decision was mistaken. The hindsight fallacy is to assume that it does."

Walker and Beckett (2005) conclude that it is vital when reviewing outcomes to recognise situations where there were risk indicators that should have been noted (a mistake was made) and situations where the significance "could not have reasonably been seen without the benefit of hindsight." (2005: 87).

Approaches to Risk/Intervention Strategies

Having considered the main approaches to risk assessment and the potential outcomes of risk assessment, we can move on to look at some of the main intervention approaches. The main intervention approaches can be categorised into:

> risk elimination
> risk reduction
> risk minimisation
> risk management

Risk Elimination

Risk elimination refers to an approach which seeks to completely eliminate risks. This is a practically impossible aim in social work and social care. There are, however, a few examples where a risk is entirely influenced by one environmental factor, where this environmental factor can be changed.

Risk Reduction

This approach seeks to "reduce" the risks or the likelihood of identified risks occurring.

Risk Minimisation

This approach is most often referred to as harm minimisation. Essentially this approach is about minimising the impact of the risk.

Risk Management

Risk management approaches seek to "manage" risks rather than attempting to eliminate them. Risk management strategies (e.g.: around substance misuse) are usually devised on a case by case basis using aspects of risk reduction and harm minimisation.

Risk Compensation

It is widely accepted that people adapt their behaviour based on their perceptions of risk. For example, where people feel that they face significant risk, they will ensure that they employ safety conscious behaviours. Where people feel 'safe' in the knowledge that risks are minimised, their behaviour will adapt to their perception of risk such that they may place themselves at heightened risk. People are in essence lulled into a false sense of security. This is widely demonstrated in research relating to road safety – for example, cyclists wearing helmets will take more risks because they feel 'safe' wearing helmets.

In devising risk management strategies, it is important to address potential behaviour changes created by risk compensation. As a straightforward example – many social care organisations have made a conscious decision not to provide self defence training for staff because of fear that staff will adapt their behaviour and place themselves in more risky situations. They may stay and "fight" rather than seek to leave when faced with an incidence of violence and aggression when in fact leaving is always the safest and most preferable option. Keeping safe is more about being equipped with knowledge and information about risk and being able to identify risk than knowing what to do in terms of self defence.

Understanding the concept of risk compensation is important in terms of discussing risk management strategies with service users. How will they ensure they contribute to the strategy through their behaviour etc?

Use the following questions in supervision discussion to explore the issues covered in this chapter.

➤ Is agency risk assessment documentation based on a clinical, actuarial or holistic approach?

➤ How might the focus of risk within assessment influence the choice of theory/models of assessment?

Explore a completed risk assessment with a student and ask them to consider true and false positives and negatives in relation to this assessment. What could be the true and false positives and negatives in this situation?

Did any recommendations in the risk assessment use the concept of defensible decision making?

E MODELS FOR INTERVENTION AND CHANGE: COUNSELLING APPROACHES

The aim in considering counselling theory and approaches is not for a social worker to become a counsellor, but the use of counselling skills is useful in any work with people. Social work is about supporting people through difficult times and facilitating change. Counselling theories give a useful framework for reflecting on the means of achieving this. The need for students to apply knowledge about change is mentioned in the QAA Benchmark Statement for Social Work (in DoH *Requirements for Social Work training* 2002:7). This refers to "the nature of social work practice" (which links back to theories about what social work is and does), and "skills in working with others". If discussion about change is to be anti-oppressive and students are to enable and empower people to make informed decisions about their own lives, counselling theories offer a sound approach to supporting people to do this.

The topics covered in this section are:

➢ Counselling Theories
➢ Rational Emotive Behaviour Therapy and Cognitive Behavioural Therapy (CBT)
➢ Brief Solution Focused Therapy (BSFT)
➢ Psychodynamic Approaches
➢ Transaction Analysis (TA)
➢ Karpman's Drama Triangle
➢ Narrative Approach
➢ Behaviourist Theory

FURTHER READING

This Guide provides an introduction to the main theories of social work. For further more detailed information on the areas covered in this section, see the following:

- Craig, Y. (ed) (1998) *Advocacy, Counselling and Mediation in Casework: Processes of Empowerment.* (London) Jessica Kingsley.
- Dryden, W. (2006) *Counselling in a Nutshell.* (London) SAGE.
- Feltham, C. and Horton, I. (2005) *The Sage Handbook of Counselling and Psychotherapy* (London) SAGE.
- Mearns, D. and Thorne, N. (1999) *Person Centred Counselling in Action.* Second Edition. (London) SAGE.
- Miller, L. (2005) *Counselling Skills for Social Work.* (London) SAGE.
- Milner, J. and O'Byrne, P. (2002) *Brief Counselling: Narratives and Solutions.* (Basingstoke) Palgrave MacMillan.
- O'Connell, W. (1998) *Solution Focused Therapy.* (London) SAGE.
- Sedan, J. (2005) *Counselling Skills in Social Work Practice.* (Buckingham) OU Press.

COUNSELLING THEORIES (24)

We have chosen to cover aspects of counselling theories not because a student or social worker is expected to work as a counsellor, but because aspects of counselling theory can be drawn on and applied to social work in a range of ways – in forming relationships, in interviewing and assessing service users etc. This chapter introduces some of the basics of counselling theory whilst subsequent chapters in the section, cover (very basically) some of the main counseling approaches.

Person Centred Counselling

The person centred approach views the individual as the expert on their own life. Each person is fully capable of fulfilling their own potential. All a person needs to achieve their life goals is a sense of acceptance and positive regard. Unfortunately in life, positive regard is made conditional on the person living a certain way.

If an individual feels that they must live a certain way to receive conditional positive regard and these expectations are not a true expression of their individuality, then psychological disturbance occurs. The psychological disturbance will continue for as long as the person feels they have to live in that way.

Person centred counselling argues that to address this, the individual needs to enter into a therapeutic relationship which consists of three key qualities:

1. Unconditional positive regard. The counsellor accepts the person unconditionally. The person is free to express all thoughts and feelings without risk of rejection or condemnation. The person does not have to 'earn' the counsellor's positive regard.

2. Empathic understanding. The counsellor seeks to accurately understand the person's thoughts and feelings. By perceiving the world from the person's own perspective, the counsellor demonstrates that the person's view has value and they are accepted. One of the techniques used in empathic understanding is reflective questioning. The counsellor listens to the person and

to ensure they have understood them, paraphrases what the person has just said, often in the form of a question.

3. Congruence. The counsellor must be authentic and genuine. The counsellor has to be transparent and there can be no hidden agenda.

If these conditions are met, then person centred counselling claims that therapeutic change will occur. If these conditions are met in relationships the person has with other people (friends, family etc) then these relationships will be as therapeutic as one with a counsellor.

Existential Counselling

Simply put, existential counselling is about why we exist. What are our ideals, priorities and values? Once we identify these we should seek to achieve them. Existential counselling recognises that our priorities and values can change and this affects our identity. Additionally, we find ourselves living under the expectations and demands of other people's priorities and values. A well adjusted response is to recognise the complexities in our life but maintain our own priorities. However, at one time or another, many or most of us compromise ourselves and live according to other peoples priorities or values.

The counsellor's role in existential counselling is to enable the person to understand their values and ideals.

Existential theory has developed a four part framework (which the counsellor may use as a prompt). The four parts are:

1. The physical dimension of health, body and the natural world.

2. The psychological or personal dimension which includes intimate relationships with others and engaging with ourselves.

3. The social dimension of public relationships.

4. The spiritual dimension of ideals, personal philosophy and meaning.

The counsellor will seek to support the person engage with themselves in all four of these dimensions.

Students are not supposed to try to act as qualified counsellors, but some of the attitudes and skills promoted by counselling theory could be effectively used. For example:

➢ Recognise that individuals are experts on their own situation.

➢ Acknowledge that all people have the potential for personal growth.

➢ If students use empathic listening and reflective questions, they should be able to understand what the service user is seeking to convey. Additionally, it is best if the student is congruent and genuine.

➢ Adopt an approach of unconditional positive regard.

➢ There are different ways that an event in a person's life can be viewed. Students may be able to suggest to a service user a way of viewing a situation that is realistic but positive.

You could discuss these attitudes and skills with students in supervision. How challenging do they find these?

In addition to these ideas, how could the student try out certain techniques safely and with the service user's agreement? When do other workers or colleagues use counselling skills and techniques?

There is a wealth of literature on this topic so this is only the briefest of summaries. Again we would stress that students should not be practicing CBT formally, but an understanding of certain principles can be helpful. Beckett suggests (2006:61) that a 'mandate' is the key, which means the service user needs to have some agreement with what techniques the student is using and why they are using them.

Rational Emotive Behaviour Therapy (REBT) recognises that we have emotions but views strong emotional reactions as leading to mental health problems. REBT argues that strong emotional reactions are often a result of a person believing that something 'must', 'should' or 'ought' to happen. For example in response to a relationship ending a person may say "I can't go on." REBT argues that the rational response is to recognise that there may be difficulties but the person can still function.

REBT claims that people are burdened with a sense of 'musts' and 'shoulds'. However, we have a choice and individuals can select alternative attitudes that are more rational.

The counsellor's role in REBT is far more directive and can include disputing the person's view of their irrational beliefs. The aim is for the person to recognise that their irrational beliefs caused their problems (and not the initial trigger events, such as redundancy, or acquiring a disability etc). The person must develop rational alternatives so that their emotional and behavioural response still enables them to function.

Ellis' ABCDEF model (1962) is similar to the ABC model drawn from behaviourism, discussed in Chapter 31.

A = Activating Experience
B = What Beliefs the person has about themselves as a result of A
C = The Consequences to the person from A

REBT and CBT are about unpicking these beliefs, so the model then moves on to consider how individuals can:

D = Dispute the beliefs and question whether they are rational
E = Replace the irrational belief with an Effective rational belief
F = Describe the Feelings which will be the result of these

For example:

A = A person fails to get a job they wanted
B = They believe that they were not good enough, that they will never get the job they want, and that they do not do well in any interviews
C = They are then stuck in the same situation and feel anxious about
applying for any other jobs

If nothing changes, this could cause great anxiety in approaching new situations which have an assessment element, or could put the person off trying again altogether (with a resulting impact on their self esteem). However, the person can learn with support to:

D = Dispute the beliefs (that failure is guaranteed; that failure is their fault; that they will never be able to build their confidence)
E = Effective beliefs (could be someone else did better on the day, doing more research about the job, trying this out in practice in a safe environment)
F = Feelings (pride, self esteem, moving on in life)

CBT is founded on the idea that our thoughts (cognitions) have an effect on our behaviours (both positive and negative. CBT is about the service user understanding the thoughts behind their behaviour, and focuses on how people can then learn to consciously direct their behaviour.

One of CBT's key concepts is "self talk". The service user needs to understand the "voices in their head" which reinforce the irrational thinking. If this is not achieved, then "learned helplessness" is the result, where the person is no longer able to function in certain situations. The worker's role is to help them to understand this and to learn and apply other ways of thinking, so that rational thinking can direct future behaviour.

We can, at times, all have negative thoughts ("What's the point?"). When a person has so many negative thoughts that it affects their ability to relate to others or to function in life as they would wish to, then it may be that Cognitive Behavioural Therapy (or counselling) could help.

The aim of the therapy is to support the person understand their own thoughts and then to test them against events in the person's own world. Often there may be some form of 'homework' where the service user has to apply a new attitude or approach to one area of their life.

CBT recognises that we can have long term life goals (successful job, fame etc), but to achieve that goal we have to work towards it. In working towards the life goal we may have to engage in activities that we would not want to do. CBT recognises that we are willing to engage in short term disadvantage if we feel we will benefit in the longer term.

CBT requires a high level of co-operation between service user and therapists. The usefulness of CBT has been highlighted in working with individuals who have depression, anxiety disorders, obsessive compulsive disorders, psychosis and schizophrenia (eg: Bradshaw 2003 and Messari and Hallam 2003).

Motivational Interviewing

This is an applied form of CBT. It originated in services for people with drug and alcohol addictions. Staff found it difficult to engage service users and there were only a small percentage of service users who moved from their state of addiction to actively seek to end their dependency. This model (motivational interviewing) was developed and has since been widely applied.

Motivational interviewing involves the worker having an empathic, non confrontational approach. Aspects of the technique include:

➢ Education about the situation the service user is in. If they are a drug user then information should be provided about the effects of substance misuse and this should be in an accessible manner.

➢ The staff member should encourage the service user to list the benefits and costs of their present lifestyle or situation. This should be concretely expressed (written down). The benefits and cost of an alternative lifestyle (if the person were to change their behaviour) should also be listed.

➤ Exploring barriers to potential goals. The staff member should support the service user recognise that there will be difficulties but many or all of these can be addressed. Again, it is best to be as concrete as possible and list the difficulties and state how each will be overcome.

➤ Reframing past events. When discussing barriers, it could be that the service user said they "tried that before and it didn't work" or similar. Past experiences may need to be explored and viewed from a different perspective. This reframing of past events is a key cognitive (thinking or ideas) skill. For example, if a person was a drug user and they said they tried to give up before (many times) and it didn't work, then rather than the 'didn't work' being emphasised the worker could point out that the service user has shown the determination to try and that it appears to be a heartfelt goal of the service user to give up.

Like many models or applied techniques, motivational interviewing is a blend of theories and models. In this case, motivational interviewing is a blend of cognitive behavioural theory, person centred practice and counselling skills.

Motivational interviewing has been considered so useful that it is extensively used especially with looked after children (and young people leaving care), offenders and people who are homeless.

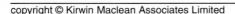

In supervision discussion ask the student what aspects of the approaches covered in this chapter might be useful in their work with service users?

Brief Solution Focused Therapy is attributed to the work of Steve De Shazer (1985) and his colleagues at the Brief Family Therapy Centre in the United States. During the early 1980s De Shazer and his colleagues considered that service users who were attending therapy needed to focus on what they wanted to achieve through therapeutic support rather than the problem that led them to seek help in the first place.

Brief Solution Focused Therapy (BSFT) has several key elements. These include:

➢ The belief that people who come to sessions due to past difficulties are able to develop strategies to address their difficulties or problems within the counselling relationship.

➢ The idea that brief intervention works as it empowers people to come up with and apply their own solutions to their presenting concerns.

➢ The need to change the focus of discussions from being dominated by problems to being built upon answers, and from experts holding the resources and power to enabling people to build on "what works" for themselves. The research says that we normally spend 50 minutes talking about problems and only 10 on solutions and this balance needs to be tipped in the exact opposite direction.

➢ The counsellor/practitioner does not focus on the past. There is more emphasis placed on the present and future.

➢ The counsellor's skills lie in asking questions that draw out the service user's strengths and skills and enables the service user to see how they can use their own skills to achieve their goals

➢ The service user – counsellor relationship is goal orientated. These goals are:

- generated by the service user
- small rather than large
- described in specific, concrete and behavioural terms
- realistic and achievable

Typical themes in BSFT sessions include:

➢ the outcomes (goals) that the service user wants to achieve

➢ the strengths and resources of the service user, including their social network

➢ identifying exceptions - identifying an occasion when all the triggers were present that could have caused the problem but the service user was able to deal with it themselves and prevent the problem occuring

➢ discussing changes in the service user's life from session to session and noting successes

➢ confirming what the strategies are that the service user finds helpful in achieving the changes

The Use of Questions

One of the skills within BSFT is the use of supportive questions aimed at enabling the service user to recognise their own strengths and abilities. Various types of questions are used, including:

➢ Goal setting questions. This is about allowing the focus at the start of a contact to be about why the service user has presented to the service in their own opinion, what they hope to achieve through their contact with the service, and how they would know that this goal had been achieved.

➢ The Miracle Question. This supports the service user identify how the future will be different when the problem is no longer present. The practitioner should shape the miracle question to be relevant to the person they are with. One aspect that is often focused on is how the service user would know or sense that the miracle (the problem they had in the past has now gone) had occurred.

➢ Scaling questions. The service user is asked to score the present on a scale of 1 to 10. The practitioner could then ask what would it take to move one point up the scale. This can also be used for identifying immediate goals.

➢ Exception finding questions. The practitioner supports the service user to identify the successful strategies they have used in the past. The intention is to give the service user the confidence to apply their own strategies to improve their situation.

➤ Coping questions. These seek to support the service user recognise the general strengths and resources they have. This approach aims to assist the service user move from an internalised problem focussed narrative to recognition of their capabilities.

BSFT has become an increasingly popular tool in social work practice. The underlying principal of this approach is that people can get preoccupied with their problems and are not able to see past them with any confidence. Workers use this approach to support service users to see past the difficulties and reframe the individual's way of looking at them. This in turn promotes a change in the way the problems are viewed and the solutions are utilised.

Use the 5 key questioning techniques above to go through with the student how a solution focused brief interview proceeds (yes, it's a role play!). Ask them to consider a relevant situation either from their placement when they have wanted support or to take on the role of a service user if they feel confident in doing this.

Ask the student how they felt at the end of this (it should only take 10-15 minutes). Discuss who they think had the power and why.

Get the student to try this with one person before the next supervision session and reflect again on how they felt using the techniques.

This is a really positive and easy theory for students to apply straight away to practice and to encourage reflection (particularly on the use of power and use of self) afterwards.

Psychodynamic theory was commonly drawn on by social workers in the 1960s and 70s. Since then its use in social work has progressively declined. It is now only really used by psychologists and a small minority of social workers. Psychodynamic theory is discussed here since some of its insights can be relevant to understanding the situation of service users.

Origins

Sigmund Freud's early development of psychodynamic theory has been developed by a number of writers. Freud claimed that we have various levels of conscious and unconscious thought. There is the ID which is the source of basic urges and the drive to survive (hence its association with sexuality). The superego is the conscious, 'public' expression that seeks to convey that we are doing what is socially acceptable. The ego was the part of the unconscious that tries to mediate between these two. The relationship between the unconscious and the conscious is a dynamic, active one. But the individual may not be (and often isn't) aware of the interactions that are occurring within themselves and engages in behaviours that are expressions of their deep unconsciousness and then seeks to rationalise them through the ego and superego.

One of the claims of psychodynamic theory is that early, negative experiences that are painful for the child are buried deep in their unconscious. However, these experiences are not lost and shape the person's relationships with the people they come into contact with from then on (although the individual may not realise what they are doing and why).

Bion (1962) developed this idea especially in terms of the main care giver and the young child. Various terms have been developed to explain the processes that occur between the young child and the primary care giver. Bion (1962) and other writers reinforce the view that the quality of relationships from early infancy onwards will shape the child's developing personality and character. If the care giver's actions (or inaction) are not adequate this will have a negative impact on the child's emotional development and their ability to engage in relationships.

One of the early themes of psychodynamic theory is that we dislike the emotional state of anxiety but are beset with it. Therefore we develop various defence mechanisms to protect ourselves from anxiety.

These defences include:

➢ Denial (claiming or acting as if an event or experience hasn't happened)

➢ Repression (memories of a bad experience are banished, present desires are suppressed e.g.: sexual desire for a person)

➢ Projection (claiming someone has an emotional state that the first person actually has, e.g.: the unfaithful man questioning his partner because he claims the partner is planning to be unfaithful)

➢ Displacement (if a person is angry with their partner, they shout at their children instead)

Freud also articulated the experience of transference. This refers to a process that occurs between the service user and the professional who is actively working with the service user. The service user transfers onto the professional emotions that have been generated as a result of past relationships. These emotions can relate to actual events in the person's past relationship or imagined (desired) event. The professional needs to be aware of the possibility of transference so they can work with it if it happens.

Psychodynamic theory argues that to understand why we do things and have the type of relationships we have, we need to look at our present emotions and actions and unpick why we are doing what we are doing. We need to understand and articulate the course or origins of our emotions and anxieties. Only by doing this can we start to consciously control our behaviour.

The counsellor or therapist has to coach, support, encourage, question assumptions, challenge etc to enable the service user to develop insight. Some therapists still use dream interpretation as a 'gateway' into the unconscious.

Implications for Social Work

Psychodynamic intervention requires long term commitment on the part of the counsellor/therapist and the service user. In modern social work most social workers cannot provide this. Clearly the social worker could recommend a psychodynamic approach if they felt the service user would benefit.

The psychodynamic approach also cautions the social worker that with some service users behavioural approaches will not work. An individual may need to do something (parent a child in a certain way, relate to their partner respectfully etc) and despite all the accepted behavioural learning techniques (role modelling, rehearsal, praise) the service user keeps relapsing. The psychodynamic response may be to say that this could be an example where the person has had very negative past experiences that are now deep in their unconscious. The person is unaware of how these unconscious fears continue to shape their behaviour today. The only way for the person to control their behaviour is to address their unconscious fears and anxieties.

There is possibly another reason why social workers may also have moved away from psychodynamic theory. It is now clear that Freud realised what was happening when young women came to him telling him of sexual encounters with their fathers. The young women were being sexually abused and raped. Freud buried this (a more sympathetic reading is that Freud was never fully sure what was happening). Instead Freud talked of children having sexual fantasies towards their parents. Arguably, this put back the protection of children from sexual abuse by 60 years. Since one aspects of Freud's early writing is wrong, it does not mean all psychodynamic theory should be rejected. However, within social work there appears to be an unconscious rejection of psychodynamic theory partly because of this.

In supervision discussion ask the student what aspects of a psychodynamic approach might be drawn on in social work today.

Transactional analysis is a framework for understanding (analysing) the communication between people (transactions). As such this theory can help explore relationships. The idea was first developed by Harris (1970) and has since been further developed by various writers (e.g.: Berne 1978, Jacobs 1999 etc).

Transactional analysis (TA) is based on an understanding of ego states and personality development. The idea is that we all have certain elements to our personality:

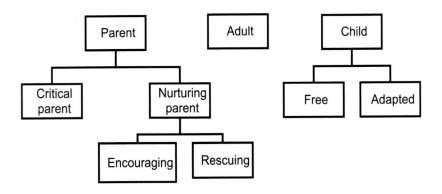

When we communicate with others, we may be "in" different states to the other person, which will impact on relationship development.

It is more straightforward to understand this using diagrammatic representation, as follows:

Appropriate Relationships

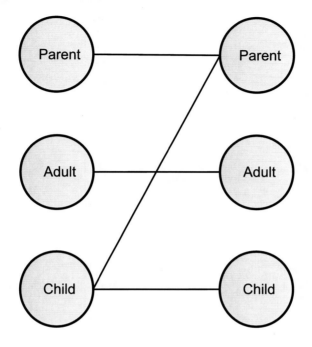

Generally complimentary relationships are evenly balanced
(represented by the straight lines). So that a parent to parent, adult to
adult, child to child relationship is appropriate. A parent to child
interaction is also appropriate and this may in fact appropriately
denote the transactions between two adults. For example, where one
person is acting in a sulky, childish manner, it might be appropriate for
the other to respond in a parental way.

Problematic Relationships

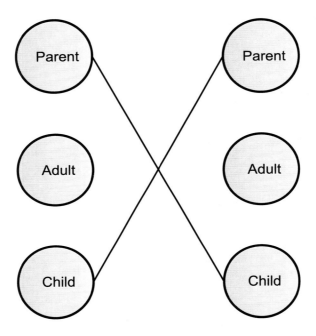

Sometimes people may experience difficulties in relating to others,
which can be as a result of their childhood, their personality or the
situation they find themselves in. For example, a service user may
feel powerless because of the power invested in the social worker –
this may lead them to respond to the worker in a child to parent
manner. The worker will want to engage with the service user on an
adult to adult basis, so there are likely to be problems in the
interactions and relationship.

Berne (1978) suggests that life experiences can 'hook' our parent and
our child which can then take over from our adult (which as adults is
the preferred state). He suggests that professionals may be able to
support service users to rehearse using their adult state in
communications more often – in this way practitioners may be able to
support service users in developing their dysfunctional relationships.

Application to Practice

Transactional analysis is a complex theory based within the psychodynamic approach. In relation to Freud, the 'parent' part of personality is viewed as the superego, the 'adult' as the ego and the 'child' as the ID. What is presented here is a simplified explanation of the approach. However, having a basic understanding of TA can help staff to recognise why people respond to them in certain ways and why they may respond to others in different ways etc. It can also help to explain why relationships may become problematic and dysfunctional.

Transactional Analysis could provide a good model for helping a student to discuss and analyse:

➤ Conflicts within families (e.g.: parenting issues)

➤ Any issues within teams, or between teams and managers

➤ Conflicts between service users and those providing care

➤ Conflicts between the team/ colleagues and workers from other agencies or disciplines

As well as helping the student to understand the conflict, an understanding of TA also brings insight about ways in which the student can deal with conflicts in discussing risk with individuals, and justifying ethical decisions to service users, managers and other agencies.

In discussion with the student, some examples of this and some training in keeping discussions adult to adult can be helpful in current and future work.

The drama triangle is another "common sense" theory which can be really useful in supporting students to understand and analyse situations where:

➢ They find it difficult to engage service users in discussing situations
➢ Families are locked into conflicts with each other or with services
➢ The family suddenly disengage from working with the student

This was developed out of Transactional Analysis and it links with developing the ability to understand "game playing" and enabling people to solve problems collaboratively as adults.

Karpman's drama triangle (1969 in Orriss 2004) suggests that people are often locked into cycles as shown:

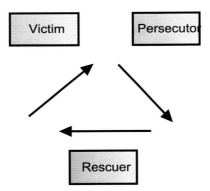

The model suggests that many vulnerable people have learned to perceive themselves as 'victims'. To be a victim requires somebody else to be the persecutor, whose behaviour towards the victim is what is creating the situation. The victim then seeks a rescuer who can come in and sort out the persecutor so that the victim is no longer subject to that oppression.

> Persecutor = Power
> Rescuer = Responsibility
> Victim = Vulnerability

The issue with this is that the victim does not have to do any changing themselves, and that often a rescuer is unable to enforce changes in the persecutor or their behaviour. When the rescuer fails to rescue the victim as is inevitable, their role as victim is re-confirmed, and the rescuer then becomes the persecutor.

This is useful as a theory because many students often enter social work training wanting to 'help people'. However, unpicking the causes of peoples' difficulties and facilitating change in every individual who is part of conflict requires the 'helper' to have the ability to stand outside a situation, and to facilitate people's ability to make their own informed choices rather than to try to rescue.

Discuss with the student a situation where they think this cycle may have occurred.

Encourage them to do further research around this and reflect upon their use of power in this situation.

Ask the student to suggest some strategies which would move their own position and that of the person they have worked with away from the triangle.

Like many theories and models discussed in this book, the narrative approach stems from a number of sources. In the UK is use is in danger of being reduced to the practice of a small number of social workers who are not in mainstream services or who defy mainstream services.

In this chapter we will give a brief overview of the narrative approach and then describe some of its uses in social work.

Overview

The narrative approach is in many ways self explanatory. It is where the social worker gives the service user the opportunity to describe their own life in their own words. This is one of the ways that the student can truly get to know the service user. The narrative approach is useful as it enables the service user to describe their own identity in the form they wish to. It also provides the service user with the opportunity to re-affirm or to redefine their identity, and it enables the person to describe themselves in a manner that includes inconsistencies, contradictions, missed opportunities, regrets, uncertainty etc.

Partly due to the time issue, it is often only utilised by workers who can devote the necessary time.

1. One of the main applications of the narrative approach is in promoting anti-discriminatory practice. The opportunity for the person to self define their identity has been seen as a vital aspect of empowerment in work with Black and Asian service users. The narrative approach is also viewed as enabling service users to understand some of the pressures they have faced and the impact that discriminatory experiences have had on them. Through the social worker's questioning, the service user could learn to realise that the oppressive features in their life were external to themselves. The worker's role is to enable the service user to reframe their life experiences, possibly by deconstructing some of the person's life events. However, it is not unusual for service users to be very aware of the nature of the discrimination and inequality they have experienced. Often one of the key

aspects is having a professional affirm the unfairness and to validate the service user's sense of oppression.

The narrative approach has also been used in feminist social work (e.g.: Reissman, 2000) and in work with adults with mental health problems (e.g.: Ridgeway, 2001).

2. It is not unusual for service users to adopt a narrative approach in their ordinary contact with social care workers or social workers. Professionals can sometimes resent the time that service users take to answer a question. The social care professional can label the service user's discussion as 'rambling' or 'off the point'. In many ways the service user could be (unconsciously) engaging in an act of resistance against social work practices that seek to reduce service users to manageable time slots or processable assessment forms.

The social worker visits the service user with their assessment form and wants an answer that neatly fits into the boxes they have on their form, but people's lives are not compartmentalised easily. The service user who gives long answers is (unconsciously) conveying that their lives have breadth (multi layered or complex) and have a depth (time). When they reduce their experiences to "fit the form", it strips them of their personality and identity.

When a person goes through a period of change (and usually a professional is involved because the service user has found the changes demanding on their personal resources) they often need time to absorb what some of the consequences are for them now. Some people require the time to talk round a subject or personal experience in order to absorb it. The narrative approach can be helpful to enable the person to adjust to their new situation.

Potentially, the narrative approach still has a lot to offer social work. Unfortunately, it is not used a great deal partly because it does not sit easily with requirements for 'mass production' of social care or social work requirements to complete neat assessment forms.

Students often have the time and opportunity to explore different ways of working as they are there to learn from practising what works. Students' learning about anti-oppressive practice could be developed by trying out the narrative approach in order to ensure they start from the service user's own individual perspective. They could then reflect on how this felt for them and the service user, and how long using the approach took versus outcomes in supervision afterwards.

We have included behaviourist theory at the conclusion of this section, since it is linked to many of the counselling theories discussed in the section. However, it also links to theories covered in the other sections of the guide as the behaviourist 'school' is so extensive (see following diagram). The basic precepts of behaviour theory have been applied in a variety of ways. Each specific application has got its own name and approach. Some 'classrooms' of the behavioural school are described in this section but this listing is not exhaustive.

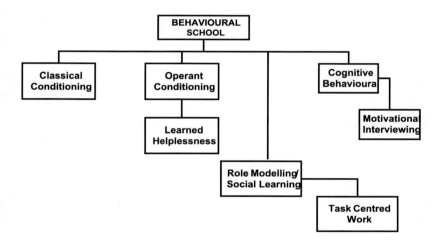

Classical Conditioning

This is most well known through Pavlov's experiment where dogs were given food at the same time as a bell was rung. After a short while, the dogs would salivate when the bell was rung even though no food was presented. The application of classical conditioning to social care is relatively limited, though there are instances where staff could come into contact with this approach. One example is where a child who persistently wets the bed may have a sensor under the groundsheet of the bed. When the sensor detects urine, a buzzer or alarm sounds. This wakes the child. After a short while the child should wake when their bladder is full without the need to urinate in bed.

Operant Conditioning

This has had a significant influence in psychology and in one form or another is used regularly in social care.

Skinner (1971) was one of the original researchers but his approach has been further developed. Operant conditioning recognised that the environment (both human generated and natural) has an effect on our behaviour.

One of the insights of operant conditioning is that it highlighted many behaviours occur randomly (we just do something or say something from out of the blue). Whether we do it or say it again will be strongly influenced by the response that we get. If we get little or no response, we may not do it again.

One example is a young child who says "I want to kill myself". This can shock a child's parents. The young child may not have any idea how to commit suicide and may not fully understand what they are saying, but whether the child says it again could be dependent on how the parents or adults around the child respond to the comment.

Operant conditioning also highlights that most behaviours are a response to a stimulus. To try to capture the processes involved in how behaviour is influenced or shaped the A:B:C continuum was developed.

'A' stands for 'antecedent' – an event happens and as a result the person engages in a behaviour, 'B', which is a response to 'A'. Immediately, or soon after the behaviour, the consequences (C) occur.

ABC charts have commonly been used in social care services. Many services have developed ABC charts so that they try to understand the broader environment a person lives in.

It is through operant conditioning that knowledge around behaviour being shaped by rewards has been developed. Rewards (or reinforcers) should be identified that the person actually likes and values. The reward should be:

> applied consistently

> given as immediately as possible after the desired behaviour occurs

If part of the reward is intrinsic to the person (internal sense of pride, achievement etc) then this is helpful. Many rewards are external to the person and can include the full range of rewards we all like, such as:

> money or gifts

> social companionship/praise

> activities the person likes

Some activities lend themselves to having rewards that automatically follow on e.g:. preparing food or drink where the reward is the enjoyment of the food or drink.

Potentially social praise and companionship is a significant reward and this should not be under estimated.

Where a desired behaviour is complex or demanding, breaking it down and having rewards that are provided for each stage should result in the behaviour being achieved.

It can be helpful to break down with a student why they think somebody is performing certain behaviours through using an ABC analysis. This could support the student to consider what "reinforcers" there are for a particular behaviour, and how the person and those around them could be supported to change these. Positive parenting programmes are an example which apply this methodology.

F

MODELS FOR INTERVENTION AND CHANGE: APPROACHES TO SOCIAL WORK

A range of theories address the way social work is practiced. This section explores some of these theories and models.

This section is both about the theories of "what a social worker does" and theories about "how to do social work." Some of the methods and models in this section are part of the student's "toolkit for practice." Other aspects are about key skills the student needs to demonstrate and link to expectations of competence from the National Occupational Standards for Social Work (TOPSS 2003).

Reading this section, you will learn more about:

➤ Group work theory
➤ Advocacy models
➤ Community work
➤ Systems theory
➤ Family group conferencing
➤ Crisis intervention
➤ Task centred practice

FURTHER READING

This Guide provides an introduction to the main theories of social care. For further more detailed information on the areas covered in this section, see the following:

➢ Bateman, N. (2000) *Advocacy Skills for Health and Social Care Professionals.* (London) Jessica Kingsley.

➢ Burford, G. and Hudson, J. (2000) *Family Group Conferencing: New Directions in Community Centred Child and Family Practice.* (New Jersey) Aldine Transaction.

➢ Dominelli, L. (2006) *Women and Community Action.* (London) Policy Press.

➢ James, R. and Gilliland, B. (2005) *Crisis Intervention Strategies.* Fifth Edition. (Belmont, CA) Brooks/Cole.

➢ Kanel, K. (2003) *A Guide to Crisis Intervention.* (Pacific Grove, CA) Brooks/Cole.

➢ Lindsay, T. and Orton, S. (2008) *Groupwork Practice in Social Work.* (Exeter) Learning Matters.

➢ Marsh, P. and Doel, M. (2005) *The Task Centred Book.* (Oxon) Routledge.

➢ Twelvetrees, A. (2001) *Community Work.* Third Edition. Practical Social Work Series. BASW (Basingstoke) Palgrave.

GROUP WORK THEORY

32

Group work theory is important in social work since many services utilise group work. Working with groups is addressed in unit 8 of the National Occupational Standards (TOPSS 2003). Unit 8 is often creatively considered by practice assessors, students and programmes generally, such that it may be that a student works with a sibling group to meet Unit 8 for example. This wouldn't necessarily be seen as formal 'groupwork' but theories of groupwork can still be useful to draw on.

Group work theory can be separated into two parts. The first is describing what is going on in terms of relationships within the group (group dynamics). The second aspect is the benefits and disadvantages of group work.

Groups are used in services for a number of reasons, including:

➤ Services may form groups because group care is easier and cheaper than individual care. A care home where there are more than two people is effectively drawing on group work. Many day centres and day services provide group care.

This type of group care is at risk of having significant tensions. Group work works best when the group has some voluntary aspect and there is a strong shared need or aim. Group care is often an expression of the service's need for a smooth running routine and so service users can't be said to volunteer for the group. The shared needs are often quite broad e.g.: a group of looked after children in a care home or older people with confusion in a day centre.

➤ Group work for meeting educational or learning needs. Where several service users have similar learning needs then group learning can be a more effective approach than one-to-one learning. Group members may prefer the social aspect to group learning.

➤ Group work dynamics are part of an intensive learning process. Some agencies intentionally use group work because group work is likely to be more successful in achieving the goal of behaviour change. Examples include agencies that set up groups for people who offend; parenting programmes; groups for people who have a drug or alcohol addiction etc. Part of the group work process is to engage in mutual critical evaluation. In other words, if a drug user is engaging in denial then other members of the group will be able to point it out, as they won't be fooled.

➤ Group work can be a key part of the process of empowerment. One of the key ways that oppressed individuals can counter discrimination is for people from the marginalised group to join together, recognise their common experiences of discrimination and to jointly take action against the discriminations. Group members can also gain from having their identity positively valued and receiving mutual support.

Group Dynamics

There have been many writers who have discussed group processes and group dynamics. Arguably the most famous is Bruce Tuckman who coined the phrase "Forming, storming, norming and performing" (Tuckman 1965).

In Tuckman's theory, the stages refer to:

Forming. This is concerned with how the individual members of the group start to orientate themselves to the group. The individuals test out boundaries in respect of leaders in the group and other group members. New relationships of dependency and interdependency are started.

Storming. This is a period of conflict around interpersonal matters and perspectives. The conflict is a form of resistance to the group and resistance to achieving the group goal. Groups can go through the 'storming' phase more than once, especially if new members join.

Norming. This is the stage in which the conflict is successfully addressed. The group develop its own identity, individuals are able to express themselves and the new roles are accepted.

Performing. In this stage, the group actually starts to successfully work towards the group task. The energy of group members is now

spent on achieving the group goals. Individual roles in the group can
become more flexible and functional.

In 1977 Tuckman and Jensen added a fifth stage.

Adjourning. This relates to the end of the group and the end of roles
that individuals had in the group. This stage highlights that
individuals can experience a sense of loss when a group finishes.

Tuckman's account of the stages groups go through has been
extensively referred to. It should be recognised that not all groups go
through these stages. However, many people involved in group work
feel Tuckman's account is useful and can be commonly seen in group
processes.

Benefits and Difficulties of Group Work

Groups often form when individuals have something in common and
the task is so significant that people realise it could be beneficial to
form a group. In social care the 'common theme' that the service
users have often relates to having a similar identified need.

The benefits of group work include:

➢ Individuals can have a sense of relief that they are not the only
ones in a certain situation. Whether it is parents trying to manage
teenagers or adults with a drug or alcohol dependency, meeting
with people in a similar situation generally gives individuals a
sense that they are not alone. The individuals can also feel able to
express themselves fully, since they are with people who, broadly
speaking, understand their situation. This too can be a source of
relief and release.

➢ Individuals can learn from other group members techniques for
dealing with a particular difficulty (using a role modelling/ social
learning approach). Sometimes comments from other group
members are respected more than comments from professionals
(who may not have experienced what the group members have
lived through).

➢ Individuals can develop a positive role and feel able to contribute.
This means the individual is no longer in a dependency
relationship; there is an equality or mutual dependency to the
relationship.

> Group members can develop insight or reflective thinking.
  Effective group work involves openness to being challenged.
  Comments from other group members can be the means by which
  individuals realise why they have recurring difficulties or are not
  progressing. Comments from group members can often be better
  received than comments from professionals. Some types of group
  work expect group members to be critical of each other (e.g.: in
  groups for people with drug or alcohol dependency).

> Group membership can help individuals develop a positive sense
  of identity. This is partly related to the first point but more creative.
  People who are ordinarily in a minority can find great benefit from
  meeting with people who have a similar identity. People from
  specific minority ethnic communities can gain much mutual support
  from meeting together to celebrate their shared identity. It can also
  be beneficial for various service user groups e.g.: teenagers
  leaving care, self-advocates who have a learning disability etc.

> Attitude change is notoriously difficult to achieve. Group work is
  considered one of the methods that is most likely to result in
  attitude change. This can be significant when the group consists
  of, say, sex offenders.

The difficulties of group work include:

> Attitude change. Sometimes groups are used to change attitudes
  'the wrong way'. Some extreme groups use group process to
  advance their own goals.

> Societal inequalities are mirrored in the group. Group work is
  intended to be a safe forum in which group members can address
  the problems they face. However, it is easy for groups to have
  within them the same prejudices and barriers that are found in
  wider society. In a group with men and women, do the men
  dominate the group and make comments that undermine the
  women? In a group that has only one black person, is that person
  at risk of being excluded?

  There are various means to counter this. One is the establishment
  of ground rules which explicitly bar sexism and racism, but group
  members then need to enforce the ground rules themselves.
  Where there is a group facilitator, they have a responsibility (along
  with group members) to raise concerns about discrimination that is
  occurring in groups.

Sometimes groups are specifically formed for people with similar identities and backgrounds e.g.: a mental health group for Asian women, to try to avoid this happening. Even then, however, there can be dominant individuals who may need aspects of their behaviour addressing since they can have a negative impact on the group.

➤ Group work has limits. Group work is intended to be beneficial for all people in the group. However, some individual members may not find the group that helpful. Group work nearly always involves an element of compromise. Group work seeks to address shared needs; on the whole it does not address individual needs that are experienced by only one group member.

In adult day services and residential care homes, groups are often formed for social activities. However, one person in the group may not want to do the planned activity. Such an individual can be viewed as awkward. Labelling such an individual as awkward or selfish is not helpful. In many ways the 'awkward' person is conveying that they are an individual and they are only in that group because that is the way services work.

In assessing the student's competence against Unit 8, how do they manage group processes and show understanding of Tuckman's model?

How does the student manage difference within and how do they ensure participation is voluntary?

Other aspects around group work which the student needs to consider could include:

➤ Managing the environment

➤ Planning and risk assessing activities

➤ Explanation of activities

➤ Evaluation and feedback as to how well activities and groups have met individual's needs

Considering these will enable the student to meet other competences alongside unit 8. Ask the student which theoretical frameworks they have drawn on in considering these arrangements.

ADVOCACY

33

Advocacy is a widely accepted principle of good practice. In many ways, though it now has a significant history within services, advocacy is often implemented in a half-hearted way with a lack of real commitment from services and staff teams. There is a clear recognition within the National Occupational Standards for Social Work (Key role 3) that awareness of the role of advocacy and direct skills in the area are key to competent social work practice (TOPSS 2003).

Essentially, there are two different forms of advocacy:

Self Advocacy

This is where the individual refines the skills they already have to speak for themselves; often self-advocates join together to form groups, both to gain a sense of personal support and to have more of an impact on the services they receive.

Self advocacy is about enabling and empowering people to act on their own behalf. There is no doubt that this is a powerful way of helping people achieve independence, although it might not be feasible for all service users. Often assertiveness training is needed, helping people raise their confidence and sense of self-worth, and teaching the skills necessary to make other people listen.

Many services now have self-advocacy groups. If staff limit their understanding of self-advocacy to the people who are members of such groups and to the topics discussed in the group they misunderstand the aim of the whole advocacy movement. People should be listened to as they express their views and make decisions about their own life and the services they receive on a day to day basis.

It is the failure of staff and services to listen to people, ordinarily, that has resulted in the rise of the self-advocacy movement.

Citizen Advocacy or Professional Advocacy

This is also known as independent advocacy. This is where an individual enters into a partnership with a service user with the intention to clearly express what the person is communicating. Citizen-advocates are usually volunteers (unpaid). However, increasingly advocates are employed by advocacy services – hence the term professional advocacy.

It is not the job of the citizen-advocate (or professional advocate) to say what they think is best for the person they have got to know. Their task is to convey what the service user is trying to say even if they disagree with what the person is saying.

Independent advocacy is important because most service users find themselves compromised in one way or another in terms of expressing their own views:

➢ There is a strong power imbalance in favour of the authorities

➢ Individuals may be lacking in confidence

➢ They may not have the verbal or other communication skills to express clearly their own meaning

➢ Their families may not agree with their own views and may put pressure on the person

An advocate can help someone work out exactly what they want, if necessary and then challenge services on that person's behalf.

Sometimes confusion reigns as to who can be an advocate. Strictly speaking, any person working for an organisation providing services or goods to an individual cannot act as that person's advocate. This is because an employee unavoidably has competing loyalties. Also, some of us find it hard not to impose what we think is best for the service user, and would genuinely struggle to present the service user's own views as paramount. We need to recognise this and allow someone else to take on that role on behalf of the service user.

The Limits of Advocacy

One of the central dilemmas of advocacy has been that a citizen advocate or professional advocate requires the service user to express their view. This raises two questions. Why does that person

---

need an advocate? and (more importantly) what about service users who cannot express themselves clearly? To answer the first question, the service user who can express themselves needs an advocate either for reasons of moral support or because services haven't listened to the service user up to now.

The more important second question has received various answers. Some advocates feel that they can identify what a person is seeking to communicate even if they have no clear language. The advocate will observe the service user and try and gauge from the service user's facial expression, body language and any vocal sounds or simple words what the service user likes and dislikes. Sometimes the advocate will draw information from people who know the service user well (family members, direct care staff) and this will be used to create as full a picture as possible. By spending time with the service user and observing them (this is sometimes called a "watching brief"), the advocate hopes to be able to get to a position where they feel they can express something of the service user's viewpoint.

Some advocates argue that such a "watching brief" is open to interpretation by the advocate and so decline to be involved.

We are left with the situation that some very vulnerable people, who don't have clear communication skills, are left almost completely voiceless.

Ask a student to consider the advantages and disadvantages of self or citizen advocacy in relation to a service user they are working with.

Ask a student to consider when they might and might not be in the best position to act as an advocate for a service user. How do they feel where they conclude that they are not in the best position to act as an advocate?

Almost 50 years ago the Younghusband Report (1959) identified that there were three main approaches in social work – individual casework, group work and community work. Following this report, community work developed considerably as a model of social work practice. However, in the 1990s community work in the UK became more sidelined as a social work/social care approach and the emphasis moved to individual case work with some group work. Perhaps the exception to this is Scotland, where community work has consistently been a popular approach.

It is interesting to note that in many other European countries and in most other continents, community work has remained an influential method of social work. With an increasing interest in International Social Work and a number of overseas recruits into the profession, ideas around community work are once again being discussed in the social work arena.

It could be argued that community work is once again becoming more popular with social inclusion initiatives such as the Surestart programme. The National Occupational Standards for Social Work (TOPSS 2003) also make regular reference to work with communities.

A range of theories are used within community work practice. Community work tends to focus on two main areas – social issues (including social inclusion, social justice etc) and education. The chosen theory base generally depends on the focus of the particular work. There are however, a range of models and approaches which are common to both social and educational community work agendas.

Thomas (1983) identified five main approaches involved in community work:

➢ Community action
➢ Community development
➢ Social planning

➢ Community organisation

➢ Service extension

Community Action

This approach is about promoting collective awareness –
encouraging action to challenge structures and systems which might
oppress or disadvantage communities. Thomas argues that in
working with communities practitioners should strive to help people
develop critical perspectives about the "status quo" and to change the
balance of power.

Community Development

This is about promoting self help, community integration and mutual
support. The idea is that neighbourhoods capacities for problem
solving will be developed.

Social Planning

This is about assessing community needs and issues and planning
strategies to meet the needs identified. Social planning involves
developing a true understanding of communities and mobilising
appropriate resources.

Community Organisation

This focuses on ensuring the collaboration of different community and
statutory agencies to promote and action joint initiatives.

Service Extension

This is a specific strategy which seeks to extend agency operations
and services by making them more relevant and accessible. This
includes extending services into the local community and giving these
services and the staff who are responsible for them, a physical
presence in the neighbourhood (Smith 2006). This is currently being
developed in practice through the roll-out of Children's Centres and
extended schools.

Capacity Building

Whilst Thomas's ideas remain influential, other strands to community work have more recently been developed. For example, ideas about capacity building emerged in the 1990s.

Skinner (1997) defines capacity building as development work designed to strengthen the ability of community organisations and groups to develop their own structures, systems and resources so that they can better define and achieve their own objectives. Groups and organisations should be supported (through training and other development activities) to be able to engage in consultation and planning, to manage community projects and to take part in partnerships and community enterprises (Skinner 1997: 2).

Participation and Empowerment

In a Joseph Rowntree Foundation research report, David Wilcox (1994) highlights the importance of community participation and empowerment in community work. He outlines 10 key ideas about community participation, which in many ways mirror the approaches outlined by Thomas (1983):

1. Level of participation – Wilcox identifies a "ladder" of levels of participation. (see later)

2. Initiation and process – participation doesn't just happen, it needs to be initiated and should have a clear process.

3. Control – the person/organisation initiating participation is in a strong position to decide how much control to give to others and how much to keep themselves.

4. Power and purpose – Wilcox highlights the importance of community workers understanding empowerment, power and powerlessness.

5. Clarity about the role of the practitioner – practitioners need to continually review their role in community work: could people in the community take on aspects of the role?

6. Stakeholders and community – anyone who has a stake in what happens is a "stakeholder". Some stakeholders will have more influence than others in communities. This should be recognised in any community initiative.

7.   Partnership – Wilcox asserts that partnership is a much abused
term. Partners must trust each other and share some
commitment. Achieving partnership takes time.

8   Commitment – people are committed when they want to
achieve something and when clear processes for partnership
and empowerment are in place.

9.   Ownership of ideas – people are more likely to be committed if
they have a sense of ownership.

10.   Confidence and capacity – people may need training to develop
confidence.

Ladder of Participation

The most influential aspect of Wilcox's work is the ladder of
participation. He suggests a five rung ladder of participation relating
to community development and community work more widely.

➢   Information – which involves merely telling people what is
planned (for their community).

➢   Consultation – this involves offering a few options and listening to
feedback, new ideas are not allowed.

➢   Deciding together – this involves encouraging additional options
and ideas and providing opportunities for joint decision making.

➢   Acting together – this involves various parties working in
partnership not only to decide on what action should take place –
but also to carry the action out.

➢   Supporting independent community interests – this involves local
groups and organisations being provided with support (which
may or may not include the provision of funds) so that they can
develop their own agendas.

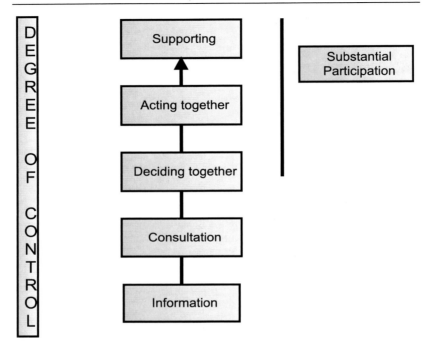

Wilcox points out that information giving and consultation are often presented as being participation. He argues that community participation and effective community work practice involves more than the simple provision of information.

Animation

Literally taken, the word "animation" means bringing something to life. This approach which originates in France, is about bringing life to communities. Animation is predominantly used in community work by those with a focus on education. However, its popularity in community development more generally is growing.

Animation is basically about motivation. Working with an animation approach practitioners try to motivate communities, using a range of methods:

copyright© Kirwin Maclean Associates Limited

"Animation is that stimulus to the mental, physical and emotional life of people in a given area which moves them to undertake a wider range of experiences through which they find a higher degree of self-realisation, self-expression and awareness of belonging to a community which they can influence."

(Smith 1999)

Practitioners using an animation approach are referred to as animators or animateurs. They often employ techniques of experiential education and community arts.

Timescales

Understanding the approaches needed in community work means acknowledging that it is a long term process:

"Community development takes time. Disadvantaged communities have to be persuaded to participate and their natural suspicion leads them to hang back until there is something to show."

(Glass 2005 in Smith 2006)

Whilst many students probably won't have the opportunity to engage in community work, there are a range of applications to everyday practice. For example, understanding the ladder of participation can help in recognising methods of engagement and partnership at any level. It can also help to understand how whole communities can experience aspects of exclusion, in any work with individuals. Ask the student to consider the ladder of participation in relation to their work.

As a practitioner working with individuals, having an understanding of community development methods can also help the student where they may be able to refer people to particular community projects.

SYSTEMS THEORY (35)

Like many theories, systems theory has at its heart a straightforward claim. For systems theory one of the key starting points is that no person is an island. Everyone has contact with other people. Some of the people are family, some friends and others are people who represent an organisation. The relationships we have with all these people and organisations form a web (or system) around us. The system around us should sustain us and enrich us. There should be a sense of harmony, balance or smooth working in our system.

Systems theory recognises that a person's support network can be placed under strain because of a change in circumstances. This change may be a new event (e.g.: acquired disability of the service user or close family member) or the change could be something progressive. The new or increased strain results in the system not working smoothly. By mapping a person's whole system, the professional should be able to work out the source of the system overload. To enable the system to operate smoothly, an individual or agency may need to be introduced (either short or long term) to balance the system again. In this way, systems theory is not personal. It does not seek to label the service user or family members.

The Social Care Institute for Excellence suggests that systems theory is relevant to social work because:

➢ It describes and explains the recurring patterns of behaviour found in families, groups and organisations.

➢ It concentrates on the relationship between the parts rather than parts in isolation.

➢ Linear thinking, a straightforward cause and effect approach, is a common approach to analysing problems. Systemic thinking, however, offers a different perspective. It suggests there are multiple causes and effects involved and we are actively involved as a part of the problem and its solutions.

(SCIE 2004:18)

In their work on systems theory Pincus and Minahan (1973) suggested that society and people operate within three systems:

➢ Informal systems that include family, friends, neighbours and work colleagues; these provide advice and emotional support and also contribute to our sense of worth and personal functioning.

➢ Formal systems that include clubs and societies, trade unions and other types of groups that can provide support.

➢ Public systems including the police, council and local government services, hospitals and schools. These systems tend to have service related functions and duties and powers in their delivery to the community.

It can be suggested that when people are experiencing difficult or traumatic times they will turn to public systems for support and assistance to help them overcome the problems. Systems theory offers the view that when people are confronted with challenges which they are not able to resolve within their support system they experience conflict and difficulties.

This is the stage at which social workers may intervene and support people to address their presenting needs. Through direct work and applying a problem solving and supporting approach social workers can develop a plan and design and implement services through effective partnership working with the service user.

The requirement is for the practitioner to assess the underlying problems and what has led to them being manifested. This will also include the need to consider the personal issues, structural forces and any disadvantage that the service user has experienced.

Pincus and Minahan (1973) also developed a framework for practitioners to use within the helping relationships to resolve the difficulties. The model highlights the need for the social worker to locate the cause of the problem and what impact the problem is having on the system.

The model refers to four aspects of the system and any intervention.

➢ The "change agent system". This refers to the social worker and the agency they are representing.

> The "client system" focuses on the service user and their system.

> The "target system" makes reference to the desired outcomes.

> The "action system" is the work that is agreed between the service user and the social care practitioner to resolve the identified issues.

An alternative way to view systems theory is to focus on the aspect of balance. The worker draws up a list of difficulties the service user is facing as well as positive aspects of their life (e.g.: supportive relationships). If the list of difficulties or problems is longer than the positive aspects, then the worker needs to introduce more positive aspects to try to re-establish a balanced system.

Systems theory is not without its critics, and commentators have suggested that it ignores the diversity of black and minority ethnic communities because it does not address the causes and effects of structural inequality.

However, systems theory is useful since it does express a basic human truth. We all rely on others to one extent or another. By looking at people's systems (support networks) we are able to recognise the strengths that people have.

Systems theory has been applied in several services. For example:

> Family therapy services have placed significant value on seeing the family as a whole and considering how they interact with each other within their family system.

> In adult services, systems theory has been extensively used to maximise support for people. Often this focuses on immediate family (carers) and the involvement of health and social care professionals or services to either fill gaps or to sustain relationships (service user/carer relationship) that are under strain.

> In learning disability services, systems theory is at the heart of person centred planning. Services should cultivate the opportunity for the service user to establish a range of informal and formal systems.

> It is helpful when working with children and families to view the child at the centre of a variety of systems. For example, the child is part of a family with its own structures, and the way the child is

viewed within this system is crucial to that child's development and well being. The community networks can also be mapped out and the child's access to these is again significant. Children are also part of the education system, and again the success or failure they experience within this is key to their development. If this system is failing the child, how far can a social worker go in attempting to address this, and which aspects of the system are outside of the worker's, child's and family's control? The child and family may also end up having to navigate systems such as those around health, mental health and youth justice. Each system has its own set of terminology, and its own values, norms and expectations. It is helpful to see these various systems as interlinking circles, as the interface between the family and each system is again key to the child's development and opportunities. Systemic thinking requires the worker to see the person in the round in order to understand the impact of social and familial structures on that individual. Only with this understanding can a plan be formed which attempts to effect change in the areas where changes and choices are possible.

Often workers support the service user to list or draw their own support systems (this is called an eco-map). There are various benefits to this including:

➤ Conveys sense of partnership working

➤ Affirms the service users sense of identity

➤ Assists the service user recognise the support they have

➤ Assists the worker understand the systems surrounding the person

Students are likely to apply systems theory in assessment, and in formulating plans which attempt to enable the service user to make changes where these are possible.

Students are quite likely to be asked to do a genogram and/or eco-map by many practice assessors. They could also look at:

➤ Which other theories does systems theory link with and require understanding and application of?

➤ How could a pictorial representation of an individual's world and the social structures which control, disempower and support them, aid understanding (both for the student and the service user)?

➤ How does this understanding lead to a plan which changes elements of the system which are not meeting the individual's needs?

The last two decades have seen the emergence of Family Group Conferences within children and young people's services in the United Kingdom. The Family Group Conference (herein referred to as FGC) emanated from New Zealand as a practice response to concern that Maori families were experiencing discrimination in the child care system and that traditional social work responses were not meeting families' needs. FGCs can be viewed as a direct application of systems theory.

The UK organisation the Family Rights Group has championed the use of FGCs within children and young people's social services, defining family group conferencing as:

"A way of giving families the chance to get together to try and make the best plan possible for their children"

In her work on FGC, Morris (1995) offers the following commentary:

"A Family Group Conference is a decision making process - it focuses on who plans and how they plan. The model can be used in any circumstances that involve the need to plan for a child."

The definition of a family within the FGC model needs to be considered within a broad context. This needs to recognise the diversity of relationships that occur within families and the tendency amongst many families to have increased contact and support with relatives during difficult times (McGlone et al, 1998).

Within the context of the Children Act 1989 and subsequent legislation there is a clear legal definition of who has parental responsibility for their children. This needs to be considered and assessed when a social work practitioner is planning to use the FGC model as a method of support and intervention.

The FGC model is all about power. Central to the practice of FGCs is the notion that all families are capable of making decisions about their needs, no matter how complex the nature of the family's difficulties. FGCs are principally aimed at enhancing and encouraging the effective functioning of families. This is uniquely achieved by integrating the families' strengths and utilising them within a problem solving process, which can also be seen as a mechanism for supporting self determination. This clearly links with solution focused methodology.

The aim is that families are given the opportunity, space, power and resources to "do it for themselves." The model works to provide children and young people with a voice via a trained advocate (either someone who the child already knows and trusts who is supported to take on that role, or a practitioner who is brought in just to perform that function). FGC works on the premise that young people should be present for all discussions concerning them, and that younger children or those who are not able to participate for the whole meeting should be supported so their views are represented.

FGCs are usually held in community venues (e.g.: church hall or community centre) so that the meeting feels different from one held in an office environment. This is crucial in bringing services to the family as a physical manifestation of the transfer of power in decision making. Services offer support but it is up to the family to decide which support they will access, as long as their plan keeps the child safe. The family decide where the meeting will be, who to invite, and what refreshments they require. Food and drink is seen as crucial to helping people feel relaxed and comfortable.

FGC aims to shift the expert, resource and professional power away from those representing agencies, so that the family are enabled to plan for themselves. The model works along the lines of the Children Act 2004 as a "best practice Team Around the Child" in increasing co-ordination of service delivery, improving communication between families and services, avoiding duplication, and having a clear basis of informed consent to share information. Families can negotiate with the Co-ordinator of the meeting if there are any issues which they do not wish to be shared openly at the FGC (or "exclusions"), again as long as none of the issues are vitally important to the planning for the child.

Marsh and Crow (1998) highlight the ways in which the FGC model seeks to address the issue that traditional social work responses to families often fail to engage wider family members. Extended family can be an "untapped resource" for social workers and the FGC model enables families to access support from within their own networks by

copyright© Kirwin Maclean Associates Limited

having extended family participate. Family and kinship members can use the FGC experience as a forum for learning about strengths of their members and mechanisms for supporting each other on a practical and emotional level.

Marsh and Crow also focus upon the ways in which FGC is a culturally sensitive approach as each family's conference will differ according to the family's needs and wishes. These differences could be around the family choosing the venue (often a community venue so that traditional power connotations around "offices" are avoided), allowing children and families to agree and own the ground rules for the meeting, and celebrating diversity (e.g. by allowing religious preference to be incorporated into the introduction of the meeting). The evidence base supports effective anti-discriminatory practice with families from black or minority ethnic communities as it validates families' own social and cultural values, (Tapsfield 2003 and Burford and Hudson 2000).

<u>The FGC Model</u>

The FGC process can be broken down into 5 key stages:

➢ Stage 1 (Referral) - there needs to be an identified need and consequently a plan to address the presenting needs. At this stage a co-ordinator is appointed who is independent of the family and the social care agency. It is also important to consider the cultural needs of the family.

➢ Stage 2 - The co-ordinator, in consultation with the child and family, issues invitations, agrees the venue, date and timing of the family meeting. The co-ordinator also prepares the participants.

➢ Stage 3 - At the start of the meeting the co-ordinator chairs the information sharing. Professionals explain their roles, responsibilities, any concerns and available resources

➢ Stage 4 - Private planning time for the family. The co-ordinator and professionals withdraw whilst the family agree a plan, which should include a contingency plan and review arrangements.

➢ Stage 5 - The co-ordinator and professionals rejoin the family/kinship and hear the plan. Resources are negotiated and the plan is agreed.

It is relevant to note that the plan should not place the child or young person at any risk, the plan should address the concerns and lead to an improved outcome and support plan to ensure the well being and development of the child/young person. Therefore, it is agencies' responsibility to own their feedback to families in the Information Sharing part of the meeting, and the Co-ordinator needs to prepare agencies to consider summarising strengths and concerns in writing so that this part of the meeting is focused. Agencies also need to "state the bottom line" in this part of the meeting, so that families know what their plan has to include to be satisfactory.

It is recognised that Family Group Conferences should not be used during sexual abuse investigations within the family due to the risk of collusion.

FGC can be used in a broad area of practice ranging from children and young people who are defined as in need (s17 of The Children Act 1989), young people leaving care, looked after children, and children and young people and their carers.

FGCs are not an alternative to Child Protection Conferences where there are issues of significant harm; it can be an effective supporting mechanism within the child protection plan or core assessment action planning.

Within some Youth Offending Services the model has been applied within the restorative youth justice process by involving the extended family in discussions about reparation and restoration towards victims after a specific offence.

Many Youth Offending Teams and other agencies that have a preventative role seek to address the underlying factors that lead to offending and to developing a plan to address the needs in a holistic manner. Working in this way, the aim is to act on the cause of the young person's behaviours, so that families can take responsibility for diverting children and young people away from the criminal justice and anti social behaviour 'career' pathway. This works in a different way from prevention interventions which rely on services to "fix the child" with work on their behaviour alone or which provide diversionary activities in isolation from the child's context.

FGCs can also be used within adult services, as the model lends itself to care planning and community care services for older people. The strengths of the model lie with the concept of partnership working, that families have the fundamental right and responsibility to fully participate in any decisions that may affect them.

There are some clear distinct practice advantages for a social worker when working with the FGC process:

➢ The approach promotes partnership and places the child at the centre

➢ Research indicates that FGCs are more successful in getting wider family participation than child protection case conferences

➢ FGCs are empowering because they actively encourage and enable the family to act as decision makers

➢ FGC is a universal model which does not have any implicit or structural discrimination base, it can be adapted and modified to meet a varying range of circumstances.

➢ The approach promotes participation and effective involvement and can challenge the view that society holds about social work intervention.

There has been a substantial amount of work and research which concludes that the FGC meeting promotes effective outcomes for children and young people.

Family Group Conferences are now used in more than 60 local authorities in England and Wales and in over 20 countries worldwide.

Barnardos 2006 (online) offer the following comments on the outcomes from Family Group Conferences:

➢ plans are viewed as safe by families and workers in over 90% of conferences

➢ significantly improved communication and understanding between agencies and families

➢ a reduction in the number of children who are accommodated and increased contact for children and young people with their family network and friends

Discuss the advantages of the FGC model with students.
How might they apply some of the principles of the model
within their practice?

CRISIS INTERVENTION

Within day to day practice with service users, students will encounter situations where individuals or families are experiencing traumatic times or crisis points within their lives as opposed to the everyday stresses which we all experience. There is a need for social work practitioners to understand this within the context of the helping relationship.

Some people cope well with crises on their own and do not require any intervention or services, and some people will seek support from their families or network of friends within their communities. Other people may turn to agencies for emotional and practical support in times of crisis. Each individual person will respond differently to presenting difficulties.

During a person's life they will experience a range of issues that can have an impact on them at both an emotional and psychological level. This may leave them feeling overwhelmed and unable to manage. These life stage events can be varied and may include bereavement, a break up of a relationship, abuse, violence both within the family and within the community, unemployment and child birth.

It is important to consider the definition of the term crisis. Bard and Ellison, 1974 (cited in Stepney and Ford 2000) offer the following:

"Crisis is a subjective reaction to a stressful life experience, one so affecting the stability of the individual that the ability to cope or function may be seriously compromised."

The heart of this model is that it is an approach that aims to support service users to regain control of their lives by learning or re-establishing coping skills so that they can move forward after the presenting issues have been dealt with and the crisis has been resolved. There is a clear expectation of time limited involvement.

Caplan (1965), one of the first writers to discuss crisis intervention, considered that crises have three phases:

➢ impact stage

➢   recoil stage

➢   adjustment and adaptation stage

Golan (1974) (cited in Coulshed and Orme 1998) also followed the
three stage approach but called them (somewhat unimaginatively):

➢   beginning

➢   middle

➢   end

The time frame from beginning to end is about 6 to 8 weeks. To
follow the stages could be something like this:

1.   A crisis arises and has some impact on a person. The person's
     own coping skills are overwhelmed by the current crisis. Hence
     services may become involved. The individual may experience a
     series of feelings and emotional responses which lead them to
     feel low and vulnerable. Golan, in her work identifies this as the
     "active crisis ".

     At this stage it is important for the social worker to understand the
     emotional responses that are being displayed by the service user.
     These could include anger, hostility, confrontation and sadness.
     The range of emotional responses will vary and depend on the
     presenting issues that have precipitated the crisis.

     The values the social worker brings into the relationship are
     crucial, given how vulnerable the service user could be. Aspects
     of professional values include:

     ➢   Most (if not all) people experience difficult times that will lead
         to a sense of vulnerability. At such times, requiring more
         support is common (and in many ways the rational thing to
         do.)

     ➢   Even though the crisis may have been unwanted and
         unexpected people have the ability for growth and
         development, a level of understanding into their own needs,
         and the ability to solve their own problems

2.   The recoil stage. This refers to the conscious, planned responses
     the service user can make. Even though the service user is in a

crisis, it is important the social worker uses a structured approach.
The worker should acknowledge that their involvement is time
limited.

3. Adjustment and adaptation/End Stage. For the service user, their
    emotional responses may still be strongly felt. However, they
    should be able to function. The need for service intervention
    should have receded, so the worker can withdraw.

Roberts (2005) in his work on crisis management and intervention
highlighted a framework that identified seven key areas for workers to
work within:

➢ Assessing lethality and safety needs

➢ Establishing rapport with the service user by using counselling
   skills (communication, a non-judgmental approach and respect).

➢ Highlighting the presenting problems and any previous coping
   mechanisms utilised by the service user. Evaluate the
   effectiveness of these mechanisms.

➢ Supporting the service user to deal with the anxiety and stress by
   engaging them in active dialogue in a safe environment which
   promotes confidentiality.

➢ Supporting the service user to explore the situation and consider
   what changes need to be made to enable them to deal with the
   problem more effectively.

➢ Developing an action plan. Provide constructive and positive
   feedback to the service user on their motivation to face up to the
   problems and deal with them.

➢ Follow up support or advice on services that could be available in
   the future.

Crisis intervention can be utilised by workers in a broad range of case
situations ranging from working with older people with mental health
needs to children and young people who are looked after. It can also
be a relevant method to employ with people who have experienced
trauma.

Crisis intervention approaches need to be delivered within the context
of anti-oppressive practice and person centred care. The worker

needs to be committed to promoting and enabling the service user as an autonomous and independent person.

There will of course be occasions where service users will present a risk to themselves and others. At this stage there needs to be a continuous assessment of this risk and (where appropriate) statutory intervention may be required to secure the person's safety and wellbeing.

Discussion about this theoretical approach is always useful in discussing Unit 4 of the National Occupational Standards "Respond to Crisis Situations." (TOPSS 2003).

Students often say that they have used crisis intervention as an approach simply because they define someone as in crisis. Ask them specifically how they have made use of the model. For example, which 'stage' is the service user in currently? etc.

TASK CENTRED PRACTICE (38)

Sometimes Task Centred Work is described as a theory in its own right, but really is an applied approach using behavioural theory at its core. It is focussed on problem solving and it is short term and time limited. Task centred work is often used when working with individuals who have relatively good independence skills.

Doel and Marsh (1992) offer the following interpretation of task centred practice:

"Task centred practice is a forward thinking, goal orientated approach to social work"

The focus of the relationship between the service user and the worker is one of partnership. The worker should assist the service user to identify the problems and difficulties that they are presently facing for themselves. There needs to be a clear understanding on what the problem is, as this promotes greater clarity and will focus the work. From this list the service user should be supported to identify which problems are their priorities. To maximise the likelihood that this approach will work, the service user's own priorities must be worked on.

Time should be taken to explore with the service user what the method promotes and how it can support them to develop solutions to their problems. Only a small number of problems should be identified in order to make the whole task manageable. The worker and service user should agree how each of the problems is to be addressed.

One mistake commonly made is that there is an assumption that task centred work relates to the tasks the worker has to do (e.g.: phoning other professionals on behalf of the service user) and this is not the intention. The focus should be on the service user recognising what they can do (in practical terms) and making a commitment to carry out the task. The worker can offer support during this time as appropriate, but the emphasis is upon the service user making their own changes and developing their own problem solving skills.

Task centred work expects that the worker and service user will agree a date to review progress. If limited progress is being made then this should be discussed and reflected on again as part of an active partnership between worker and service user.

One of the aspirations of task centred work is that by successfully completing a task, the service user will have a sense of achievement. This will be intrinsically rewarding as well as solving a problem in the person's own life (which will also generate a sense of benefit for the service user).

Additionally, task centred work predicts that once the person has had a problem and solved it, then the next time the same or a similar problem arises they will be able to address the problem themselves.

Task centred practice was developed by Reid and Shyne in 1969 (Higham 2006). It evolved from a general concern that in depth social work practice was not achieving the same outcomes for service users as short term intervention. It was largely developed by social work practitioners and educationalists to support the thinking that long term intervention was not as practical both in terms of the worker/service user relationship and the cost effectiveness of services. This was because it became clear that the first six to twelve weeks of professional involvement were the most productive in terms of service user responsiveness. After this 'diminishing returns' set in very rapidly, meaning that continuing progress was very gradual and sometimes minimal.

In the early part of the 1960s Perlman suggested that social case work needed to be given some recognition within the context of the emerging social work profession. A cornerstone of Perlman's work was the belief and understanding that within human development there is a need for people to set and accomplish tasks to enable them to develop effective management and coping strategies.

The model is recognised as an appropriate tool for social workers to use in the following circumstances with service users:

➤ Personal conflict

➤ Dissatisfaction in social relationships

➤ Difficulty in role performance and functioning

➤ Emotional reactions to a stressful life event

➤ Limited resources, poverty, poor housing, unemployment

> Behavioral problems that are not assessed as psychological
definitions

[Payne (1997), the original list was developed by Reid (1978)]

Task centred practice has five key stages that are often referred to as
phases (Ford and Postle 2000). These phases should be followed
within a structured approach to appointments or sessions with service
users and workers should plan for no more than 12 meetings.
However, this will depend on the progress and the presenting
problems that the service user is looking to overcome.

The stages can be broken down into the following key sections in
direct work to support service users to achieve their goals:

1. Problem Exploration. The social worker and the service user use
   this time to discuss the problems and consider which issues they
   want to deal with first.

2. Agreement. There should be a shared understanding between
   the service user and practitioner about what the problem is and
   how they are going to target and action plan. This phase is also
   referred to as the selecting and prioritising of problems.

3. Formulating an objective. This phase involves setting goals and
   making a contract between the worker and service user. The
   contract should also reflect the arrangements for the worker and
   service user to meet with deadlines. Care should be taken by the
   worker to ensure that the problems that have been identified to
   work on do not overwhelm the service user. They should be
   achievable and realistic.

4. Achieving the tasks or working to implement the tasks. This can
   be done jointly with the service user in a session or separately.
   There is also the potential for the worker to undertake any
   identified advocacy work here.

5. Bringing the work to a conclusion. This is an opportunity to
   consider what progress has been made and discussion should
   focus on the outcomes and developments that the service user
   has made towards their identified goals. This session should aim
   to be as in depth as possible and should have a reflective focus.
   The worker may also want to ask the service user how they feel
   about the problems now, and what changes have been made.

It is important to remember that if the presenting issues have been resolved the sessions can be finished earlier. However, in the event of the issues not being resolved or of further problems emerging the worker and the service user can agree to meet for some more sessions. Again, these should be time limited.

The Limitations of Task Centred Practice

There is a wealth of evidence that suggests that task centred practice as a method of intervention is effective and is a tool that is understood by service users (Reid and Epstein 1972). However, as with any theoretical approach, there are limitations.

Commentators suggest that one of the weaknesses of task centred practice is that it a relatively simple model and should not be seen as the universal underpinning theoretical tool to inform direct work with service users.

Some people's emotional and life situation is complex and the task centred approach does not easily address complex emotional issues.

A psychodynamic approach would go as far as saying that if deep rooted unconscious behaviours (that are limiting a person's social functioning) are not addressed through counselling or therapy, then lists of tasks are in danger of being irrelevant. The person won't do them as they will act in ways consistent with their unconscious directions.

Some practitioners have found the drawing up of an agreement or contract problematic [stage or phase 3 in Ford and Postle's (2000) list]. It has been claimed that drawing up a contract can come across as disempowering. Since the tasks should be for the service user to do, it can come across as setting homework for the service user which will be 'marked' by the social worker (teacher) the next time they meet. Counter arguments to this suggest that the agreement or contract ensures there is clarity and entering into agreements (of some form) is commonly done by adults (e.g.: job contract). However, the criticism does have some merit.

Task centred practice is often misunderstood by workers. It is commonly assumed it is the worker who does all the tasks (e.g.: contact the local housing agency). The worker's task is to support the service user to recognise that they have the skills or to support them

to develop the skills and confidence to do the task for themselves.
When the service user does this, it is self reinforcing (both in terms of
an issue or problem is resolved and they did it themselves).

In spite of its limitations, task centred practice is likely to be a staple
theory in the practice of many social care and social work staff.

When a student suggests that they have applied task-
centred principles, the two key questions are HOW? and
WHY? Our experience indicates that students may say that
they have used a task centred approach but in subsequent
discussion, they are not really able to say in what way.

For example, what were the factors which made them decide
that a task-centred approach would work?

How did they explain this to the service user and gain
agreement to work in this way?

How did they follow the model Ford and Postle suggest?

What are the timescales and what will the student do if the
changes they have identified are not occurring?

How did they ensure commitment was agreed to the tasks
which were agreed?

What level of support did they agree to offer in the interim
(and have they been empowerment orientated)?

G AN ECLECTIC APPROACH

We have tried, in this Guide, to provide a framework for practice assessors to easily refer to specific theoretical approaches, using Sibeon's distinction (1989) to group the theories.

The theories could easily have been grouped together differently. For example, you will find that there are common themes amongst many of the theories in different sections.

No single theory can ever provide a clear explanation about a service user's situation, along with an appropriate and failsafe plan of action, so practitioners generally take an eclectic approach to their work most of the time. Essentially being eclectic means using a range of theories in any given situation.

Students often say that they have used an eclectic approach in a situation. This final section will help to explore just what this might mean.

ECLECTICISM

The concept of eclecticism is essentially about using a range of different theories. It often involves using only parts of each theory in a kind of "pick and mix" fashion. In our view, all social work professionals use an eclectic approach to the application of theory to practice. This is really the only effective way to work, in that no single theory provides a clear explanation of a service user's situation along with an obvious, failsafe plan of action. The situations which social workers deal with are complex and each one is unique. As such, service users have a right to expect an approach tailored to their particular situation which draws on the best that a whole range of perspectives have to offer.

Lehman and Cody (2001) provide a useful framework for what they term a generalist eclectic approach. They assert that there are five major elements to this approach:

1. A person-in-environment perspective that is informed by ecological systems theory

2. An emphasis on the development of a good helping relationship that fosters empowerment

3. The flexible use of a problem-solving process to provide structure and guidance to work with clients

4. A holistic, multi-level assessment that includes a focus on issues of diversity and oppression and on strengths

5. The flexible/eclectic use of a wide range of theories and techniques that are selected on the basis of their relevance to each unique client situation

(Lehman and Cody 2001: 6)

We would add a sixth element to this – the importance of viewing the service user as the expert on their own situation. This is a common element of many modern social work theories and fits well with the current 'personalisation' agenda.

Lehman and Cody's model (2001) demonstrates that taking an eclectic approach is more than just using a couple of different theoretical perspectives in a given situation.

In our experience, an understanding of an eclectic approach to social work theory is helpful in working with students for a few reasons:

➤ Students may say that they are using an eclectic approach as an "easy answer" to a challenging question on the use of theory.

➤ Students sometimes believe they must use a theory in its purest sense, following it precisely. Often this is not possible, for a range of reasons. The theory may need to be adapted and the "best" and most appropriate parts chosen for use. A range of other (possibly adapted) theories may need to be used alongside the original theory of choice. This is essentially taking an eclectic approach. Students may find this complexity confusing and difficult and may need reassurance about this.

➤ Most professions make use of an eclectic approach in their work. Social work, as an ever increasingly complex profession, is no different.

If a student says they have used an eclectic approach, try discussing the five elements of the generalist eclectic approach proposed by Lehman and Cody. Which of these elements do they think they have used? How?

Ask a student in what ways an eclectic approach is more than being able to name two or three potentially relevant theoretical approaches.

INDEX

REFERENCES

Ainsworth, M., Blehar, M., Waters, E. and Wall, S. (1978) *Patterns of Attachment: A Psychological Study of the Study of the Strange Situation.* (Hillsdale) Erlbaum Associates.

Bandura, A. (1977) *Social Learning Theory.* (Englewood Cliffs, New Hersey) Prentice Hall.

Barnardos (2006) *Family Group Conferences.* (online at www.barnardos.org.uk/familygroupconferences.htm - accessed 1.11.06)

Beckett, C. (2006) *Essential Theory for Social Work Practice.* (London) SAGE.

Belsky, J. and Cassidy, J. (1994) *Attachment: Theory and Evidence.* In M. Rutter and D. Hays (Eds) *Development Through Life: A Handbook for Clinicians.* (373-492pp) (Oxford) Blackwell Scientific Publications.

Berne, E. (1978) *A Layman's Guide to Psychiatry and Psychoanalysis.* (London) Penguin.

Bion, W. (1962) *Learning from Experience.* (London) Heinemann.

Bowlby, J. (1969) *Attachment and Loss, Volume I. Attachment* (London) Hogarth Press.

Bowlby, J. (1973) *Attachment and Loss, Volume II. Separation: Anxiety and Anger* (New York) Basic Books.

Bowlby, J. (1980) *Attachment and Loss, Volume III. Loss: Sadness and Depressions* (New York) Basic Books.

Bradshaw, J. (1972) *The Concept of Social Need.* New Society 496. pp640-643.

Bradshaw, W. (2003) *Use of single system research to evaluate the effectiveness of cognitive-behavioural treatment of schizophrenia.* British Journal of Social Work, 33, pp 885-899.

Brandon, D. (1997) *The Trick of Being Ordinary.* (Cambridge) Anglia
Polytechnic.

Burford, G. and Hudson, J. (eds) (2000) *Family Group Conferencing:
New directions in community-centred child and family practice.* (New
York) Aldine de Gruyter.

Burton, J. (ed) (1990) *Conflict: Human Needs Theory.* (London)
Macmillan.

Caplan, G, (1965) *Principles of Preventative Psychiatry.* (London)
Tavistock.

Carson, D. (1996) *Risking Legal Repercussions.* in Kemshall, H. and
Pritchard, J, (ed) Good Practice in Risk Assessment and Risk
Management (Volume 1). (London) Jessica Kingsley Publishing pp3-
12.

Coulshed, V. and Orme, J. (1998) *Social Work Practice: An
Introduction.* (Basingstoke) Palgrave.

Cousins, N. (1989) *Head First: The Biology of Hop.e* (New York) E.P.
Dutton.

Cross, W. (1971) *The negro to black conversion experience: towards
the psychology of black liberation.* Black World 20, pp.13-27.

Cross, W. (1980) *Models of psychological nigrescence: a literature
review.* In R. Jones (ed) Black Psychology (New York) Harper Row.

Cross, W. (1991) *Shades of Black: Diversity in African American
Identity.* (Philadelphia) Temple University Press.

Department of Health (2002) *Requirements for Social Work Training.*
(London) DOH.

De Shazer, S. (1985) *Keys to Solution in Brief Therapy.* (New York)
Norton.

Doel, M. and Marsh, P. (1992) *Task Centred Social Work.* (Aldershot)
Ashgate.

Doel M. and Shardlow S. (2005) *Modern Social Work Practice: Teaching and Learning in Practice Settings.* (Aldershot) Ashgate Publishing Limited.

Dominelli, L. (2002) *Feminist Theory.* In Davies, M. (Ed) The Blackwell Companion to Social Work. (Oxford) Blackwell.

Dutt, R. and Phillips, M. (2000) *Assessing black children in need and their families.* In Assessing Children in Need and their Families: Practice Guidance, Department of Health (London) The Stationery Office.

Ellis, A. (1962) *Optimizing Rational Self Talk for Health, Happiness and Wellbeing.* (online at www.lifeskillstraining.org/cog_restructuring. Htm – accessed 2.3.08).

Erikson, E. (1950) *Childhood and Societ.y* (New York) Norton.

Festinger, L. (1957) *A Theory of Cognitive Dissonance.* (Stanford) Standford University Press.

Ford, P. and Postle, K. (2000) *Task centred practice and care management.* In P. Stepney and D, Ford (eds) Social Work Models, Methods and Theories (Dorset) Russell House Publishing Ltd.

General Social Care Council (2002) *Codes of Practice for Social Care Workers and Employers* (London) GSCC.

Glendrinning, C., Hirst, M. and Harris, J. (2005) *Understanding and Measuring Personal Social Services Outputs Relating to Disabled Adults and Carers.* (York) SPRU University of York.

Harris, J., Foster, M., Jackson, K. and Morgan, H. (2005) *Outcomes for Disabled Service Users.* (York) SPRU. University of York.

Harris, T. (1970) *I'm OK – You're OK.* (London) Pan.

Heider, F. (1958) *Attribution Theory.* (online at www.12manage.com/ methods_Heider_attribution_theory.html - accessed 12.2.08).

Higham, P. (2006) *Social Work. Introducing Professional Practice.* (London) Sage Publications.

Honey, P. and Mumford, A. (2000) *The Learning Style Helpers Guide.*
(Maidenhead) Peter Honey Publications Limited.

Howe, D., Dooley, T. and Hinings, D. (2000) *Assessment and
decision making in a case of child neglect and abuse using an
attachment perspective.* Child and Family Social Work, 5, 143-155pp.

Hylton, C. (1997) *Family Survival Strategies.* (London) Exploring
Parenthood.

Jacobs, M. (1999) *Psychodynamic Counselling in Action.* (London)
SAGE.

Keley, H. (1967) *Kelley's Convariation Model.* (online at
www.everything2.com/index.pl?node id=1398834 – accessed
16.2.08).

Kemshall, H. (2002) *Risk Assessment and Management.* In Davies,
M. (ed) The Blackwell Companion to Social Work (Oxford) Blackwell.

Knowles, M. (1984) *The Adult Learner: A Neglected Species.*
(Houston) Gulf Publishing.

Kolb, D.A. (1984) *Experiential Learning.* (Englewood Cliffs, NJ)
Prentice Hall.

Kubler Ross, E. (1969) *On Death and Dying.* (New York) Macmillan.

Lehman, P. and Cody, N. (2001) *Theoretical Perspectives for Direct
Social Work Practice: A Generalist Eclectic Approach.* (New York)
Springer Publishing Company.

Limandri, B. and Sheridan, D. (1995) *The prediction of intentional
interpersonal violence.* In J. Campbell (ed) Assessing
Dangerousness: Violence by Sexual Offenders, Batterers and Child
Abusers. (London) SAGE.

Macdonald, K. and Macdonald, G. (1999) *Perceptions of risk.* In
Parsloe, P. (ed) Risk Assessment in Social Work and Social Care.
(London) Jessica Kingsley.

Marsh, P. and Crow G. (1998) *Family Group Conferences In Child Welfare*. (Oxford) Wiley-Blackwell.

Maslow, A. (1970) *Motivation and Personality*. (New York) Harper Collins.

McClelland, D. (1961) *The Achieving Society*. (Princeton) Van Nostrand.

McGlone, F., Park, A. and Smith, K. (1998) *Families and Kinship*. (York) Joseph Rowntree Foundation.

Messari, S. and Hallam, R. (2003) *CBT for psychosis: A qualitative analysis of clients experiences*. British Journal of Clinical Psychology, 42, pp. 171-188.

Milner, J. and O'Byrne, P. (1998) *Assessment in Social Work*. (Basingstoke) MacMillam.

Monahan, J. and Steadman, H. (1994) *Violence and Mental Disorder: Developments in Risk Assessment*. (Chicago) University of Chicago Press.

Morris, K. (1995) *Family Group Conferences: An Introductory Pack*. (London) Family Rights Group.

Mullender, A. (2002) *Persistent oppressions: The example of domestic violence*. In Critical Practice in Social Work, R. Adams, L. Dominelli and M. Payne (Eds) (Basingstoke) Palgrave MacMillan.

National Institute for Mental Health in England (2003). *Inside Outside: Improving mental health services for black and minority ethnic communities in England*. (Leeds) Department of Health.

Neufeldt, A. (1990) *Celebrating Differences*. Journal of Practical Approaches to Developmental Handicap, 15, pp 3-6.

O'Brien, J. (1980) *An Ordinary Life*. (London) Kings Fund Centre.

Orme, J. (2002) *Feminist Social Work*. In Social Work: Themes, Issues and Critical Debates. R. Adams, L. Dominelli and M. Payne (Eds) (Basingstoke) Palgrave/Open University.

Orris, M. (2004) *Karpman Drama Triangle.* (online at www.coaching supervisionacademy.com/our_approach/karpman_drama_triangle.pht ml – accessed 2.1.08).

Ossana, S., Helms, J. and Leonard, M. (1992) *Do 'womanist' identity attitudes influence college women's self esteem and perceptions of environmental bias?* Journal of Counselling and Development, 70, pp.402-408

Owusu-Bempah, K. (2002) *Culture, Ethnicity and Identity.* In M. Davies (ed) The Blackwell Companion to Social Work (Oxford) Blackwell Publishing.

Owusu-Bempah, K. and Howitt, D. (1999) *Even their soul is defective.* The Psychologist 12.

Payne, M. (1997) *Modern Social Work Theory: A Critical Introduction.* (Basingstoke) Palgrave MacMillan.

Phillipson, C. (1998) *Reconstructing Old Age.* (London) SAGE.

Piaget, J. (1928) *Judgement and Reasoning in the Child.* (London) Routledge and Kegan Paul.

Pincus, A. and Minahan, A. (1973) *Social Work Practice: Model and Method.* (Itasca) Peacock.

Reid, W. (1978) *The Task Centred System.* (New York) Columbia University Press.

Reid, W. and Epstein, L. (ed) (1972) *Task Centred Practice.* (New York) Columbia University Press.

Ridgeway, P. (2001) *Restorying Psychiatric Disability. Learning from first person recovery narratives.* Psychiatric Rehabilitation Journal, 24, pp 335-343.

Riessman, C. (2000) *Analysis of Personal Narratives.* In J. Gubrium and J. Holstein (Eds) Handbook of Interviewing. (New York) SAGE.

Roberts, A. (ed) (2005) *Crisis Intervention Handbook. Assessment, treatment and research.* (Oxford) Oxford University Press.

Roth, R. (1989) *Preparing the reflective practitioner: Transforming the apprentice through the dialectic.* Journal of Teacher Education, 40, 31-35pp.

Rutter, M. (1995) *Clinical Implications of Attachment Concepts: Retrospect and Prospect.* Journal of Child Psychology and Psychiatry. 36 549-571pp.

Saleebey, D. (1996) *The strengths perspective in social work practice: extensions and cautions.* Social Work 41, pp296-305.

Schon, D. (1987) *Educating The Reflective Practitioner.* (San Francisco) Jossey Bass.

SCIE (2004) *Leading Practice: A Development Programme for First Line Managers.* (online at www.scie.org.uk/publications/leading practice/files/SCIE Participant's HB.pdf – accessed 1.11.06)

Sibeon, R. (1989) *Comments on the structure and form of social work knowledge.* Social Work and Social Sciences Review, 1 (1) pp.29-44.

Simmering, M. (2008) *Attribution theory.* (online at www.referencefor business.com/management – accessed 13.2.08).

Skinner, B.F. (1971) *Beyond Freedom and Dignity.* (Indianapolis) Hackett Publishing Company.

Skinner, S. (1997) *Building Community Strengths: A Resource Book on Capacity Building.* (London) Community Development Foundation.

Smale, G., Tuson, G., Biehal, N. and Marsh, P. (1993) *Empowerment, Assessment, Care Management and the Skilled Worker.* (London) HMSO.

Smith, M. (1999) *Animation.* [online www.infed.org/animate/b-animat.htm accessed 9.12.06]

Smith, M.K. (2006) *Community Work.* The Encyclopaedia of Informal Education [online www.infed.org/community/b-comwrk.htm - accessed 8.12.06]

Social Care Institute of Excellence (2003) *Learning and Teaching in Social Work Education: Assessment.* (London) SAGE.

Stepney, P. and Ford, D. (eds) (2000) *Social work Models, Methods and Theories.* (Dorset) Russell House Publishing.

Sutton, C. (1999) *Helping Families with Troubled Children.* (London) Wiley.

Tapsfield, R. (2003) *Family group conferences: family-led decision making.* Childright 195. p16-17.

Taylor, B. and Devine, D. (1993) *Assessing Needs and Planning Care in Social Work.* (London) Arena Press.

Thomas, D. (1983) *The Making of Community Work.* (London) Allen and Unwin.

Thompson, N. (2005) *Anti-Discriminatory Practice* Third Edition (Basingstoke) Palgrave.

Thompson, N. (1998) *Promoting Equality.* (Basingstoke) Macmillan.

Thompson, N. (2005) *Understanding Social Work: Preparing for Practice.* (Basingstoke) Palgrave Macmillan.

Topss England (2003) *National Occupational Standards for Social Work.* (Leeds) Topss England.

Tuckman, B. (1965) *Developmental Sequence in Small Groups.* Psychological Bulletin, 64, 384-399pp.

Tuckman, B. and Jensen, M. (1977) *Stages of small group development revisited.* Group and Organisational Studies, 2, 419-427pp

Vanier, J. (1988) *The Broken Body* (London) Darton, Longman and Todd Limited.

Vygotsky, L., Vygotskii, L. and Kozulin, A (Eds) (1934/1986) *Thought and Language.* (Cambridge, Massachusetts) The MIT Press.

Walker, S. and Beckett, C. (2005) *Social Work Assessment and Intervention.* (Dorset) Russell House Publishing.

Weiner, B. (1974) *Attribution Theory.* (online at www.tip.psychology
.org/weiner – accessed 16.2.08).

Wilcox, D. (1994) *The Guide to Effective Partnership.* (online
www.partnerships.org.uk/guide - accessed 1.12.06).

Williams, P. (2006) *Social Work with People with Learning Difficulties.*
(Exeter) Learning Matters.

Wolfensberger, W. (1983) *Social role valorization: A proposed new
term for the principle of normalization.* Mental Retardation, 21, 234-
239pp.

Wolfensberger, W. (1988) *Common assets of mentally retarded
people that are commonly not acknowledged.* Mental retardation, 26,
pp 63-70.

Wolfensberger, W. and Thomas, S. (1983) *PASSING (Program
Analysis of Service Systems' Implementation of Normalization Goals):
Normalization criteria and ratings manual.* (Toronto) National Institute
on Mental Retardation.

Younghusband, E. (1959) *Report of the Working Party on Social
Workers in the Local Authority Health and Welfare Services.* (London)
HMSO.